MW01147139

Working Congress

Media and Public Affairs

Working Congress

A Guide for Senators,
Representatives, and Citizens

Edited by Robert Mann

Louisiana State University Press
Baton Rouge

Published by Louisiana State University Press
Copyright © 2014 by Louisiana State University Press
All rights reserved
Manufactured in the United States of America
LSU Press Paperback Original
First printing

Designer: Michelle A. Neustrom
Typeface: Sentinel
Printer and binder: Maple Press

Library of Congress Cataloging-in-Publication Data

Mann, Robert, 1958–
  Working congress : a guide for senators, representatives, and
citizens / edited by Robert Mann.
    pages cm. — (Media and public affairs)
  ISBN 978-0-8071-5737-4 (pbk. : alk. paper) — ISBN 978-0-
8071-5738-1 (pdf) — ISBN 978-0-8071-5739-8 (epub) — ISBN
978-0-8071-5740-4 (mobi) 1. Political culture—United States.
2. Political parties—Unied States. 3. United States. Congress.
4. Partisanship. 5. Courtesy—United States. 6. Right and left
(Political science)—United States. I. Title.
  JK1726.M37 2015
  328.73—dc23

                                                    2014006077

The paper in this book meets the guidelines for permanence
and durability of the Committee on Production Guidelines for
Book Longevity of the Council on Library Resources. ∞

Contents

Working Congress

Introduction

Robert Mann

There are few legislative battles more dramatic and inspiring than the debate and passage of the Civil Rights Act of 1964 and the Voting Rights Act of 1965—among the most significant and controversial laws of the twentieth century. Their enactment came after decades of struggle and strife in the streets and byways of the nation—from New York to New Orleans, Boston to Birmingham—and on the National Mall in Washington. During the civil rights struggle, the chambers and committee rooms of Congress were also stages for acrimony and conflict. Members of Congress fought bitterly over proposed civil rights legislation from the early 1940s through the late 1960s and even into the 1970s.

Eventually, Congress acted and passed the historic bills. That's why the civil rights story is not merely about a movement in the streets; it is the story of the triumph of compromise and conciliation in Congress. The civil rights laws of the 1960s offer us some of the best examples of what is possible when political leaders transcend partisan political differences and consider more than just the immediate judgment of voters. The civil rights acts were moments when many members of Congress—with the judgment of history in mind—put their reelection at risk.

Looking at these bills with fifty years perspective, in a time when Congress seems paralyzed and unable to act on any bill that is remotely controversial, it is not unreasonable to ask if today's Congress could debate and pass the same civil rights bills. The question is hypothetical in many respects, but it may be useful as we consider what afflicts the current Congress.

Or perhaps there are better questions: Could the current Congress tackle and eventually enact legislation addressing any sort of controversial, emotionally packed issue such as civil rights? Could the congressional leaders of 2014 conduct themselves with the sobriety, dignity, and statesmanship of Everett Dirksen, Hubert Humphrey, Lyndon Johnson, Robert Kennedy, and Mike Mansfield? It seems that these questions are not difficult to answer. Indeed, it's almost impossible to imagine that the story would play out in the same way should current members of Congress be magically transported back to 1964. The Washington that we know today is thoroughly infected with partisanship. Its leaders are acutely focused on short-term political aims and influenced or controlled by lobbyists and political consultants. It is impossible to imagine current members of Congress mustering the bipartisan cooperation and trust necessary to pass such controversial and politically volatile legislation.

Many years ago, when examining the passage of these bills for a history of the civil rights movement in Congress, I was struck by the almost absolute absence of pollsters and political consultants from the equation. When political leaders such as Dirksen, Humphrey, Johnson, and Kennedy met to negotiate the details of the civil rights laws, they did so without political consultants whispering in their ears. They negotiated without benefit of daily tracking polls guiding them on every nuance of the legislation. Of course, political considerations were not far from their minds. They framed their support or opposition in ways designed to be most appealing to their constituents. But they were not slaves to the polls. Upon signing the 1964 bill, Johnson reportedly told an aide that he was probably signing away the South in presidential politics for a generation. He was correct, of course, but he signed the bill nonetheless, strongly suspecting the cost to him and his party. He and many members of Congress believed that history would judge them more kindly than their constituents. They were certainly wise in taking that gamble.

It may not, however, have been such gamble. These leaders enjoyed what many politicians today have never experienced—a degree of latitude from the passions of their constituents to conduct business in ways they believed best for the nation. They, especially senators, did not fear immediate retribution by the voters (that is, after all, one reason the Senate was created). The compromises they forged on civil rights and other bills were usually in private and reached only after considerable negotiation—not over social media or cable television. And they compromised with ideological opponents who in many cases were also longtime friends and neighbors.

There was no C-SPAN, Fox News, MSNBC, or CNN featuring pundits and counterfeit journalists shouting insults and analyzing only the political ramifications of the bills, not their substantive details. Civil rights supporters marched in the streets and loudly picketed Washington, but it was often the violent reaction to those protests—in Birmingham, Jackson, Montgomery, and Selma—that moved public opinion toward support of the bills. To the extent that proponents and opponents of civil rights were organized to express their views to Congress—and they were very well organized on both sides—the expressions were generally heartfelt demonstrations of opinion, not the poll-driven and consultant-manipulated declarations of what political operatives now call "grassroots lobbying" or "issues management."

Perhaps, despite all the current impediments to passage of controversial legislation, the Congress of today could indeed act and pass the civil rights bills. As Everett Dirksen said at the time, quoting Victor Hugo, nothing can stop an idea whose time has come. Yet it is difficult to imagine these bills, in the current political environment, passing with any significant degree of dignity or high-mindedness among most members of Congress. This is not to say that the debates in 1964 and 1965 were always dignified and responsible, but the worst behavior by southern racists was aberrant and often denounced or ignored by both sides in the debate.

Perhaps most significant—and, sadly, quaint—was the truly bipartisan nature of the civil rights bills. Leaders of both parties believed that these laws were best for the country and for the health of their political parties; they willingly cooperated to ensure their passage, rarely attacking each other in public or in private during an arduous and politically perilous process (especially in 1964, in the midst of congressional and presidential elections).

Nothing would have threatened passage of these bills more than an ugly, partisan battle between Democrats and Republicans; nothing ensured their success more than the willingness of political leaders to set aside their political weapons in pursuit of the most significant social reforms since the abolition of slavery. To suggest that something similar could happen today is fantasy. As journalist Robert G. Kaiser observed in his 2013 book, *Act of Congress: How America's Essential Institution Works, and How It Doesn't:* "Very few members or challengers overrule the strategies of their political consultants. Legislating is no longer the principal preoccupation of our legislators—politics is."[1]

The story of the civil rights bills is not simply a tale of legislative battles of old; it is the story of what may be a lost era when statesmanship was possible and when progress was achieved in ways that united the country and appealed to our highest principles, not our basest instincts. The era was far from perfect. Its leaders were deeply flawed in many ways. Yet compared to the deplorable state of affairs in Washington today, the 1960s were a relative age of enlightenment.

One way to gauge this shift is to examine the respect that Congress commanded among the public in the early 1960s versus today. After the 1964 elections a Harris Poll put Congress's approval rating at 64 percent.[2] By August 2012 the public's approval of Congress had sunk to its all-time low—10 percent.[3] An institution deplored by 90 percent of the U.S. public might be able to pass laws (although even that is often impossible); it cannot claim to effectively represent the American public. While individual members continue to be reelected in overwhelming numbers, most Americans have dismissed Congress as irrelevant or even harmful to their well-being. Following the government shutdown in the fall of 2013, the public's disgust with Congress only deepened. While its paralyzing partisanship and rancor may not be the only factors in Congress's staggering decline in public opinion, it is difficult to imagine exactly what could be a more significant factor. If Congress—especially the House—will ever function as the representative institution the founders intended, its members must regain the public's trust.

That said, we should also acknowledge that other periods in congressional history were far more rancorous and even violent. A cursory reading of congressional history from the early 1800s through the Civil War will shock the sensibilities of any American concerned about civility in public life. Duals, fistfights, and brutal physical attacks in the House and Senate chambers were not uncommon. So bad was violence among members that in 1839 Congress passed legislation forbidding duels within the District of Columbia.

It is, however, cold comfort to assuage ourselves with the assurance that as bad and dysfunctional as Congress has become, it could always be worse. By modern standards it could not be much worse. Congress's low approval rating is not much higher than the four- or five-point margin of error of a poll that might find *zero* pubic approval.

Therefore, with a desire to explore whether some aspects of an earlier era of cooperation and bipartisanship are possible again, the staff of the Reilly Center for Media & Public Affairs at Louisiana State University's Manship School of Mass Communication went to Washington, D.C., in May 2013. Each year in Baton Rouge the center sponsors a public affairs symposium named for former Louisiana senator John Breaux, renowned for his bipartisanship during a thirty-year career in the U.S. House and Senate. For the first time we took the Breaux Symposium to the capital and, with Senator Breaux's leadership and guidance, gathered for a daylong discussion at George Washington University about "ways to make Congress work again." We convened a group of former members of Congress and several respected congressional scholars who discussed the current state of our politics and debated what, if anything, could be done to change it for the better.

This book is the product of that symposium. From the beginning Senator Breaux's aim and ours was to produce an accessible book that could be shared with every member of Congress. We were joined in this enterprise by two valued partners: the United States Association of Former Members of Congress and George Washington University's Graduate School of Political Management. As envisioned by each of us, this book analyzes many of the problems and challenges facing Congress and offers suggestions for ending or reducing the gridlock. We are hoping that members of Congress, journalists, and citizens will read it and discover ways that they might contribute to making Congress more representative of the public's desire for less-partisan representation.

We do not pretend that this book offers solutions that, if adopted, would instantly transform Congress into a bipartisan utopia. In fact, several of the scholars who contributed to this book doubt that there is anything Congress could do in the way of rules changes and other reforms that would significantly modify the institution. It would, they say, require significant changes to our political system, and to the electorate as a whole, to significantly influence the way Congress conducts its business. In other words, they argue, it's not Congress that has grown dysfunctional; it's our political system itself that no longer works.

But we persist in our belief that men and women of goodwill can find ways to work together. Some of those ways are to be found in the wisdom passed along to us by former members of Congress who, despite their philosophical differences, managed to work together and pass meaningful legislation during their respective terms of office. Participating in the conference, for example, were two former Senate majority leaders—Republican Trent Lott and Democrat Tom Daschle —who were effusive in their praise of each other and who offered examples of times when they found common ground that led to passage of substantive legislation. The wisdom and practical advice of these former members of Congress is sprinkled throughout this volume.

In the opening chapter former Republican representative Mickey Edwards of Oklahoma, now of the Aspen Institute, argues that Congress must address how it reshapes its House districts each decade and must find a way to solve the problem of "big money." More important, Edwards says, Congress needs better leadership equipped to "deal with the most important national issues," not merely "advancing a partisan agenda and using whatever parliamentary maneuvers are available to them to thwart the advance of alternative views."

In chapter 2 Professor Ross Baker of Rutgers University offers a useful review of the various congressional reforms that have been proposed and enacted over the years. He contends that "they offer a valuable cautionary tale about efforts at structural reform in Congress," arguing that "the institutions of Congress are shaped by the larger political forces at a given time."

Professor Frances E. Lee of the University of Maryland makes much the same point in chapter 3, only from a different perspective. She explains how partisan party divides have paralyzed Congress and made it difficult, if not impossible, for leaders to forge compromises. "The bottom line is that we shouldn't have any illusions about how profoundly difficult it is to make policy in today's circumstances," she writes. "Nor should we have any illusions about just how difficult it will be to reverse the long-term transformations that have given rise to these deep and pervasive partisan conflicts."

Professor Brian L. Fife of Indiana University–Purdue University Fort Wayne argues in chapter 4 that the transformation of Congress will not occur "until members of Congress reform the manner in which they are selected by the people of the United States in the first place." Fife proposes several reforms, including publicly financed elections, greater access to the ballot, and, counterintuitively, a reinvigoration of political parties.

In chapter 5 Susan Herbst, president of the University of Connecticut, rightly scoffs at the notion that ours is the most polarized era in American history. She further argues that "perhaps incivility is overblown as a problem in American politics, and the central issue is how thin-skinned we have become in our daily social and political lives." Among other things, Herbst proposes the "extensive teaching of argument" in public schools so that "young people [can] develop their passions and then argue with force and evidence."

Finally, in chapter 6 former Republican representative Mark Kennedy of Minnesota (now director of the Graduate School of Political Management at George Washington University) examines "the hurdles that make it more difficult" for members of Congress "to persuade each other." He offers a series of commonsense, practical "solutions" to those hurdles, including reforms in congressional redistricting, campaign finance reforms requiring greater disclosure, and broadening of political coalitions to include activist groups often excluded from debates. Kennedy also applies the Wilson-Lowi Matrix, a topology of political styles, to congressional debate as a way to understand why some issues appear so intractable.

Will reading and adopting all of the recommendations in this book radically change Congress for the better? Perhaps. But as Ross Baker illustrates, today's reforms might well become tomorrow's problems. Indeed, it would be arrogant and foolhardy to declare, "These are Congress's evils, and here are the solutions." Better to acknowledge that, like the United States, Congress is an experiment and a work in progress. What we propose with this book is a greater awareness among citizens and members of Congress about the need not so much to reform or transform Congress or our political system but to help members trim their sails more often in order to keep our government institutions and therefore the nation moving in the direction most likely to restore and maintain the public's confidence in its political leadership.

Restoring—or at least strengthening—public confidence in government, so completely lacking in today's political environment, is perhaps the most important objective in any attempt to influence the way Congress goes about its business. In 1787 Benjamin Franklin emerged from the Constitutional Convention to encounter the following question from a passerby, "Well, Doctor, what have we got—a Republic or a Monarchy?" Franklin famously replied, "A Republic, if you can keep it."

I do not believe that it is overly dramatic to suggest that the maintenance of our republic could eventually be jeopardized. When and if that day comes, there will likely be more to blame than simply low public esteem of Congress. But it's also not an exaggeration to suggest that a Congress held in high esteem because it meets the needs and embodies the hopes of most Americans could well save the Republic from collapse or revolution.

To quote John F. Kennedy, "Those who make peaceful revolution impossible will make violent revolution inevitable." I hope that this book might help promote a peaceful *evolution* of Congress in the direction of becoming the representative and effective body most Americans desire.[4]

NOTES

1. Robert G. Kaiser, *Act of Congress: How America's Essential Institution Works, and How It Doesn't* (New York: Knopf, 2013), 374.

2. Louis Harris, "Image of Congress Has Improved Vastly since '64 Session Convened," *Washington Post,* January 4, 1965.

3. "Congress and the Public," Gallup, www.gallup.com/poll/1600/congress-public.aspx (accessed September 19, 2013).

4. Portions of this introduction were adapted from the editor's 2007 book, *When Freedom Would Triumph: The Civil Rights Struggle in Congress* (Baton Rouge: Louisiana State University Press, 2007).

1

What's the Problem with Congress?

Mickey Edwards

To get a clear picture of the extent of America's current governmental dysfunction, what it is that isn't working, and how dramatically these failures undermine the unique system that had been carefully devised to protect our freedoms, it's first necessary to understand what precisely America's founders did, why they did it, and how they did it. In the world the founders knew, it was the common political practice for the people to place their trust in the rule and protection of a monarch and to cloak themselves in the subservient trappings of the loyal subject. What was exceptional about the United States was the decision to turn the system on its head—to put ultimate authority in the hands of the people themselves; here they would be citizens, not subjects, and it would be they who would, through the ballot box, determine what wars they would fight and what taxes they would pay.

This was a revolutionary concept at the time, and to make this new system work—and to prove their seriousness about the matter—the founders devised a Constitution in which almost every major power of government was withheld from the executive and placed in the hands of a branch made up of citizens chosen by and answerable to the people themselves (the Congress has the final say over federal spending, taxes, going to war, approving treaties, creating federal programs, deciding who serves on the Supreme Court and other federal courts, even who sits in the president's own cabinet). Representatives answered to the people directly, and senators answered to them indirectly, being appointed by state legislators who themselves were directly elected and subject to periodic defeat if their actions did not win public approval. To further underscore their intent, the founders began the Constitution, in Article I, with a lengthy description of the many legislative powers (including the regulation of the armed forces), and only afterward did they give a short description, in Article II, to the much-more-limited role of the president.

There are at least four important lessons to be taken from this formulation. The first, and most important, is that the United States was to be a nation in which the people sent their sons and fathers (and today, mothers and sisters) to fight and possibly die in battle only if the people themselves concluded that the cause was worth the sacrifice. And that the earnings of their labor would be taken by government only to the extent the people themselves considered the benefits purchased to be equal to or more than the sacrifice required. It was because the Congress was more easily controlled by the people that it became the branch of government in which the greatest power was vested.

The second, clear not only from the purposes for which the Constitutional Convention was summoned but also from the powers subsequently granted to Congress, was that the entity that emerged, the modern United States, was to be in every sense a real nation. That meant the government was not only to be constrained in what powers it exercised but also that it was to be empowered to act in the national interest so long as the people were amenable to the policies and programs the government purported to undertake and the proposed actions did not exceed the government's constitutional authority.

Those two truths lead inevitably to a third: the powers granted to Congress are not given as a gift but as an obligation. It is not the members of Congress—and not the president—who are the true holders of the powers bestowed but the people themselves, in whose hands the nation's well-being rests. The founders placed a fearsome responsibility on the shoulders of the men and women who serve in Congress and the White House: it is through them, and more so through the

Congress, that the people exercise the sovereignty the founders recognized as their right. Failure to protect the freedoms envisioned in the Constitution and failure to carry out the legitimate functions of government are both affronts to the people themselves.

The fourth, also obvious, lesson is that none of this constitutional plan matters—it is in fact a sham—if the elections, and particularly the elections of members of Congress, do not accurately reflect the desires of the people. Partisan primaries, partisan control of congressional decision making, partisan shaping of congressional districts, and campaign finance laws that give disproportionate influence to the wealthy are not merely "problems"; they constitute a significant undermining of the entire American political process. This matters because democracy is not about policy—people of goodwill may have honest disagreements about which policies best serve the national interest—but about process. It is "how" we make our decisions—by what rules, guided by what permissions and prohibitions, pursuant to an honest election process—that determines whether we are indeed a democracy, whether we are still the republic the founders envisioned, whether we are truly America the Exceptional.

Elections

Ours is not a nation in which governance is based on majority rule. Many of the provisions in the Constitution, including those specifically enumerated in the Bill of Rights, spell out clear protections against infringements on the rights of minorities even by the most overwhelming majorities (the political system of the United States is best described as that of a mediated and constrained democracy). But if we are a democracy at all, the election process itself should reflect the majority opinion of the voters.

That, of course, is not how it really works. Because the election systems are dominated by political parties, the men and women who are elected to Congress may or may not be those favored by the major-ity of their constituents.

In states, for example, that conduct party primaries and do not provide for runoff primaries in the event that no candidate wins a ma-jority of the primary vote, candidates may be elected and serve long political careers, wielding great influence over public policy, when the majority even of their own party members preferred somebody else.[1] In Massachusetts, Congressman Edward Markey recently won a special election to succeed John Kerry in the United States Senate after Kerry stepped down to serve as secretary of state. Massachu-setts is essentially a one-party state, and winning a Democratic Party primary virtually ensures election. In 1974 Markey won his first con-gressional race by receiving 22 percent of the vote in a party primary; even 78 percent of Democrats preferred somebody else, but with no runoff and no real Republican presence, Markey won a seat in Con-gress.[2] When Michael Capuano, the former mayor of Somerville, ran for Congress, he got 23 percent of the vote in his primary and, facing no serious Republican challenge, became a congressman, voting on national policy, even though 77 percent of his own party primary vot-ers didn't want him in that role.[3] One of the most powerful members of Congress, California's George Miller, won his primary in 1974 (the same year Markey won in Massachusetts) with only 38 percent of the primary vote—which was enough.[4] So much for majority rule.

But even so, it is likely that Markey, Capuano, and Miller all are fairly representative of the political leanings of their constituents. That is not necessarily the case when low turnout in party primaries allows the election of candidates who reflect the views of the most extreme, partisan, and ideological voters in the party. This was the situation in 2010, when a popular congressman and former Delaware governor, Mike Castle, was defeated in a Republican Senate primary. His opponent, who had never held elective office, received just thirty thousand votes in a state of nearly one million people.[5] But Delaware

has what is known as a "sore loser" law, arranged by the political parties, that gives the parties de facto control over access to the general
election ballot.[6] Because Castle lost the primary, he was prohibited
from having his name appear on the November ballot, and the bulk of
Delaware voters no longer had the option of selecting him to be their
next United States senator.

The same thing happened in Utah, a state of approximately three
million people, where thirty-five hundred Republicans chose a Senate nominee in a closed party convention; of those, two thousand
voted to deny renomination to the popular incumbent senator, Robert
Bennett, and as a result, he, too, was barred from having his name on
the general election ballot—the options of three million people limited by the votes of two thousand partisans because Utah also has a
sore loser law.[7] So, in fact, do forty-six of the fifty states.[8] Voters pay
for the elections, but the parties determine the available choices, and
in a purported democracy two private power-seeking clubs are able
to deny access to the ballot. What would American leaders say about
the state of democracy in another country if the same thing were to
happen there?

Back, then, to the questions of what defines the current dysfunction in government—what is it that isn't working? And what led us to
this result?

In a government of balanced powers, with separate branches even
of the Congress and more than three hundred million citizens, "consensus" on anything substantial is nearly impossible. Progress on
any important issue requires willingness on the part of government
leaders to negotiate and compromise. Because party primaries, dominated by hyper-partisan activists, can cut short a political career (sore
loser laws create an almost insurmountable obstacle for candidates
who lose primaries to take their case to the broader electorate), legislators find themselves forced to shape their appeals not to the general
voting public but to the most rigid and uncompromising members of

their own parties. In office, in order to avoid challenges in their own party primaries, they vote to assuage the concerns of those activists—and that means refusing to compromise with, and sometimes refusing even to talk to, the "enemy." Thus, finding common ground on federal budgets, tax plans, health care laws, and almost any other of the issues that fall legitimately within the purview of the federal government becomes an ever more rare occurrence.

There is a further and even more disturbing element to this electoral system that makes loyalty to party, and to the most extreme elements of that party, the key to political success. If fealty to party requires a legislator to oppose initiatives put forth by the enemy, one is under the same pressure to support the actions of other members of one's own team. When "party" rather than position is the measure of one's political identity, members of Congress see the president not as the head of a separate branch of government, to be kept in check, but as either one's own party leader, to be supported in all he or she may propose, or as the leader of the opposition party, always to be opposed. Thus, it has become common for both Republicans and Democrats in Congress to support actions undertaken by a president of the same party even if they would object strenuously to those actions if a member of the opposing party occupied the White House. One study of support or opposition to expanded surveillance of citizens by the federal government found that when George W. Bush was president, his aggressive security initiatives were hailed by Republicans and vigorously opposed by Democrats; when Barack Obama became president, virtually the same policies were supported by Democrats and attacked by Republicans.[9]

One of the most fundamental elements of the American constitutional system is the separation of powers and the assumption that the Congress—the repository of almost all governmental authority—would jealously guard its own prerogatives and stand against any constitutional overreach by the president. Partisan politics undermines that supposition and erodes the separation between branches that was thought by the founders to be the surest guarantor of our freedoms.

Redistricting

There is yet another feature of party-driven politics that strengthens officials' loyalties to the political clubs they represent and undermines the ability to forge common ground compromises in the public interest. In nearly four fifths of the states, congressional district boundaries that shape the nature of the electorate are drawn not by disinterested citizens but by whichever party leaders have gained control of a state legislature. In states in which both houses of the legislature and the governor's office are held by the same party, the common result is for districts to be drawn in such a way as to minimize the likelihood of a serious challenge to the controlling party's candidates. This practice has been condemned by reformers who wish to see more competition for legislative seats, and it is a reasonable concern, but that's not the only, or the most important, grounds for objecting to the procedure.

One of the least remembered, and most important, provisions in the Constitution requires that every member of Congress be an actual inhabitant of the state from which he or she is elected. The purpose is clear: voters should have a reasonable amount of familiarity with those who seek to represent them, and members of Congress should be familiar with the interests and preferences of those they represent. My own experience with party-driven redistricting illustrates how that goal of representativeness can be undermined by a system that puts party interests first.

When I was first elected, I represented the entirely urban community in which I had grown to adulthood—the city in which I had attended elementary school, junior high school, and high school and

17

in which the store my father managed either prospered or lagged in step with the success of local businesses and employment at the nearby airbase. I grew up knowing the employers, the products, the sports teams, the acquisitions at the zoo, the fund-raising efforts for the local symphony orchestra. Oklahoma City was diverse, but I knew its rhythms, and the people knew me as one of their own. As the first member of my party elected in that district since 1928, I was naturally targeted by the opposition party, which then controlled the state legislature and thus drew congressional district boundaries. Unable to defeat me, the legislature redrew my district to put as many of my fellow party members in the district as possible, removing them from other districts that would then be safer for their party. As a result, I found myself trying to adequately represent small-town merchants, wheat farmers, cattle ranchers, Indian tribes—people I grew to have affection for but for whom I could be only a less-than-articulate spokesman when the issues that mattered so much to them came before the Congress for decision. The party that controlled the state legislature—both parties are equally guilty of this—put party advantage ahead of the representativeness that is the essence of a constitutional democracy.

But the point here is about the dysfunction of government; my own inability to be as good a voice for my constituents as they deserved, as bad an outcome as that is, is only one of the results of party control of redistricting. As my district shifted from urban, with a highly diverse population, to rural and much whiter, it became more conservative, and the voters in my already conservative district became even more so. And those who were most politically active and who voted in party primaries, more so still. The same scenario plays out across the country: partisan redistricting makes liberal areas more liberal and less amenable to compromise with conservatives, and it makes conservative districts more conservative and more resistant to working across party lines. Combined with closed party primaries and sore loser laws that largely restrict ballot access to those who have won the endorsement of the most partisan in their own parties, redistricting completes the driving of the stake through the heart of bipartisanship.

Money

The principal effect of party control of redistricting and ballot access is to place more power over the government in the hands of that minority of citizens who are most partisan, most ideological, and most resistant to cross-party cooperation and compromise. To a large extent, the significant influence of money on the political system has the same effect (many of the so-called Super PACs are actually run by longtime party operatives), but it also has the additional effect of magnifying the influence of men and women who use disproportionate wealth not to help a favorite political party but to skew public policy to their own benefit.

The problems of "big money" are too complicated to go into in a single chapter (there are several good books on the subject),[10] but whatever reforms are undertaken, they must ensure that our government functions as a democratic republic, not as an oligarchy, whether by limiting the size and frequency of campaign contributions or limiting the range of potential contributors (my own preference is for a system in which only individuals could make financial contributions to an election campaign—no corporations, no labor unions, no political action committees, no political parties).

In addition, the federal government can offset the effect of money by allowing candidates for federal office to run a limited number of campaign advertisements on radio and television (the airwaves are publicly owned) and to send free mailings to voters, just as members of Congress are already permitted to do. Likewise, state governments can send candidate information mailings to registered voters (some states already send such mailings with information about noncandidate questions on the ballot). These changes would not prevent some candidates from having more money to spend than their opponents but would at least mitigate the effect of the financial advantage.

Some candidates will invariably have more in the way of campaign funds than others, and deservedly so, if more people support their candidacy. The goal is not to level the playing field between candidates who enjoy public support and those who don't; rather, it's to ensure that it is "voter preference" that translates into success at the polls, not merely the preference of unrepresentative interest groups.

In the Halls of Congress

To this point I have dealt with those factors that influence who is ultimately elected to serve in Congress. But the problems do not end there.

When Barack Obama was elected president in 2008, Senator Mitch McConnell said his principal goal as Republican leader in the Senate—at a time when the nation was at war, the economy was in the doldrums, and bridges and highways were crumbling—was to defeat Obama for reelection.[11] When Nancy Pelosi became speaker of the House—with the nation at war and serious problems facing the country—she said her principal goal was to elect more Democrats.[12] The United States Congress does not have real legislative leaders whose job it is to facilitate the consideration of proposals to deal with the most important national issues; instead, leaders in both the House of Representatives and the Senate are selected, almost always on a straight party-line vote, by whichever party holds the majority, no matter how slim, and they consequently function primarily as party leaders, advancing a partisan agenda and using whatever parliamentary maneuvers are available to them to thwart the advance of alternative views.

Committees are the principal choke points in Congress—the place where bills go to die or be revised or be passed on to the entire body for a chance at becoming the law of the land. In the legislative process committees are key, and membership on a particular committee that deals with one's principal concerns—agriculture, energy, foreign policy, defense, or another—is an essential ingredient in permitting a legislator to achieve significant influence over public policy. How does one achieve those coveted positions? Every member of Congress arrives in Washington with a packet of skills, expertise, experiences, constituent concerns, political beliefs, and personal values. Every member takes the same oath of fealty to the Constitution, is fully vested with the authority of the office, and in the House represents approximately the same number of American citizens. Given this legal equality, there are many ways to make committee assignments (for example, by seniority or by a drawing if more members seek a particular assignment than the number of committee seats that are available to be filled).

Instead, despite the fact that the Constitution makes no provision for political parties and each of the first four American presidents warned against creation of the kinds of political parties we now know, it is the parties that choose who will sit on which committees. The party with a temporary majority gets to have more members on each committee, and the seats on those committees are filled by party members who raise the greatest amount of money for the party and those who pledge to stick loyally with the team on major issues (what the party can give, it can also take away, and to act independently of the party leadership is to risk losing the committee position one has worked so hard to attain). It is an outrageous system that forecloses honest attempts to seek common ground on matters that must be resolved in the national interest.

This is only a glimpse into the hard-core partisanship—the persistent seeking of party advantage—that paralyzes and destroys any attempt within Congress to find honest solutions to difficult national problems. Committee staffs are invariably partisan (Republicans analyze the budget through the assumptions of Republican staff members, Democrats through the eyes of fellow Democrats): the majority party controls the agenda and chooses which legislation will even be considered on the House or Senate floor, thwarting any alternatives that the majority party's leaders don't support. Party interests trump democracy in the governing system as well as in elections.

Solutions?

More than one fourth of the states have now acted to remove from party leaders the ability to shape congressional district boundaries on the basis of partisan advantage. Every state should do the same thing. The single greatest obstacle to creating a functional national Congress, in which party interests are secondary to national interests, is the election system itself in most states, which, through the combination of party primaries and sore loser laws, allows parties to deny access to the general election ballot to any candidate who did not win the endorsement of the partisan ideologues who often dominate primary voting. In 2006 Washington State joined Louisiana in eliminating party primaries, creating instead a new system in which all candidates run on the same ballot, regardless of party, and all voters within that constituency can choose among all of the candidates.[13] If a candidate wins a majority, he or she is elected; if no candidate wins a majority, there is a second round, with a runoff between the top two. In 2010 California followed suit.[14] With such a system political campaigns will still be hotly contested, but the winners will be those who were chosen by the majority of all participating registered voters, not merely the majority of hardline partisan activists. This, too, is a way to force elected officials to be responsive to a broader and more diverse electorate, increasing the pressure to find ways to cooperate—and to compromise when necessary—with those whose views diverge from one's own.

Today roughly 40 percent of Americans register as independents rather than as members of a political party.[15] An article in *USA Today* characterized the trend as a flight from the party system.[16] In the end that is the only way we can restore a workable Congress capable of bearing the burden of leadership imposed by the Constitution. Party membership is a fine thing—we all like to affiliate with affinity groups, people who think more or less the same way we do—but these private power-seeking clubs ought not to have the ability to limit access to the ballot, to shape the Congress to meet their partisan goals, or to block consideration of legislative alternatives. We need a Congress in which its members think of themselves, and act, as Americans, not as party loyalists. Only then will the dysfunction of recent years fade and a meeting between Republicans and Democrats to work out solutions to common problems no longer merit front-page newspaper stories and breathless reports on national television.

NOTES

1. Brian F. Schaffner, *Politics, Parties and Elections in America,* 7th ed. (Boston: Wadsworth, 2012), 133.

2. Katharine Q. Seelye, "Democrat Wins Special Election for Kerry's Senate Seat," *New York Times,* June 25, 2013.

3. Anthony Flint, "In the Long Run, Persistence Wins," *Boston Globe,* September 17, 1998.

4. "CA District 7—D Primary," Our Campaigns, www.ourcampaigns.com/RaceDetail .html?RaceID=735206 (accessed on August 29, 2013).

5. Mickey Edwards, *The Parties versus the People: How to Turn Republicans and Democrats into Americans* (New Haven: Yale University Press, 2012), 38.

6. Edwards, *Parties versus the People,* 44.

7. Edwards, *Parties versus the People,* 39.

8. Edwards, *Parties versus the People,* 44.

9. "Majority Views NSA Phone Tracking as Acceptable Anti-Terror Tactic," Pew Research Center for the People and the Press, www.people-press.org/2013/06/10/ majority-views-nsa-phone-tracking-as-acceptable-anti-terror-tactic/ (accessed on

August 29, 2013); "Proof That American Voters Are Hypocrites Whose Views Flip-Flop When Their Party Is in the White House," *Business Insider,* www.businessinsider.com /poll-nsa-surveillance-pew-research-edward-snowden-whistleblower-2013-6 (accessed on August 29, 2013).

10. The best are Lawrence Lessig, *Republic, Lost: How Money Corrupts Congress— and a Plan to Stop It* (New York: Twelve Books, 2011); and Robert G. Kaiser, *So Damn Much Money: The Triumph of Lobbying and the Corrosion of American Government* (New York: Vintage, 2010).

11. Edwards, *Parties versus the People,* 12.

12. Edwards, *Parties versus the People,* 11.

13. Edwards, *Parties versus the People,* 48.

14. Edwards, *Parties versus the People,* 17.

15. Edwards, *Parties versus the People,* 10.

16. Edwards, *Parties versus the People,* 11.

Voices of Former Members of Congress

Former Senator John Breaux (D-La.): Look what's happening in the House. Arguably, the Democratic caucus in the House has become much more liberal because of the defeat of the so-called Blue Dog Democrats. The Republicans, on the other hand, I think, arguably, have become much more conservative with the election of all of the Tea Party Republicans. So, instead of having a larger middle, both extremes of both parties have become much stronger, and it's very difficult to have a liberal Democrat agreeing with a Tea Party Republican, and the middle has become smaller and smaller.

The same thing has happened in the Senate. The middle, when I was there, we had a [John] Chafee [R-R.I.]–[John] Breaux caucus. We had at least fifteen, eighteen members. Both parties had met on a regular basis, Democrat, Republican. Now if you could get two or three, it would be an accomplishment because the middle has gotten smaller, and the two ends have gotten much stronger.

Former Senator Tom Daschle (D-S.Dak.): I think probably one of the biggest differences is the amount of time that members spend in Washington today. I often say that the airplane is a big reason why we find ourselves in the situation we do because what it has done is accommodated travel far more frequently. [Former senator] Blanche [Lincoln (D-Ark.)] was telling me she was actually criticized for moving her children to Washington. Well, it virtually doesn't happen anymore. No one moves their family to Washington, and because so little time is spent here—in fact, I think we've set the record this year [2013] so far for the fewest number of votes cast. So, I think that's one of the big differences. If you're not here, it's pretty hard to build friendships and relationships and ultimately to accommodate the kind of legislative processes required that are built on those relationships.

Former Senator Trent Lott (R-Miss.): John [Breaux] and Tom [Daschle] and I have talked a lot about the differences now and the way it used to be. I did come to Washington in 1968 as a staff member to a Democrat. It was a lot different in those days, no fax machines, no computers, no cell phones. I think members had six round-trips home a year. Members brought their families. They stayed here. Of course, the Congress, even in those days, didn't stay beyond usually, say, October. They'd go home, so their children actually went to school in their home districts, and that was a long time ago, and then, of course, fast-forward through my House years in the '70s and '80s and then in the Senate.

I think a lot of it is modern technology. You are under pressure to keep up with what's going on. Instantaneously, people can reach you all hours of the day and night. You got the 24/7 news media. If you make a mistake or if you get involved in something that you shouldn't have, I guarantee you, it will be on the news for several days running, so that's part of it.

What we really need—and I don't want to be too critical of the leaders because I know how tough their job is—but to get things done, you do have to have men and women who are willing to work together, to step up.

When I went from the House to the Senate, I was a partisan warrior. Having been the whip in the House, in the minority for sixteen years, I went in every day trying to figure out a way I could beat the other side, and after a few months I said: "You know what, this is not working. I'm not happy. I'm not getting anything done. I got to figure out how this institution works, and I got to change my attitude and try to find a way to help get some things done."

And part of it was being willing to amble across the aisle and talk to John Breaux and say, "Hey, what can we get done together?" and being willing to work with [former representative] Norm Dicks [D-Wash.] and with Tom Daschle.

Tom and I did talk a lot. Tom and I sometimes took on our conferences. I remember one time in particular, neither his caucus nor my conference was ready to go on a bill, but we knew it needed to be done, and we stepped up and said, "We're going to move this bill," and we got it done.

A second problem I'll point out is the need to have strong leadership, and it's an overused term, but regular order is really needed. Let the committees have hearings. Let the subcommittees mark up. Let the full committee mark up. Have votes. I can't believe senators don't want to have to cast a tough vote. You got a six-year term. You don't want to have to vote on immigration reform or defense issues. You go to the floor and have a full debate and then go to conference. I think they've had like one real conference maybe in the last couple of years. That's where the final work needs to be done.

One of the things that I think is really seriously wrong is so few pieces of major legislation today start in the subcommittee, go through the full committee, go to the floor, then go to the Senate, have a conference. That just doesn't happen. Things get imposed: "This is it, you got to take it like it is." And that's not the way we legislated when we were doing all that good work over in the Senate between 1968 and 1976, so it's a serious problem.

2

The Ascent of Bipartisanship to the Congressional Reform Agenda

Ross K. Baker

There is a cottage industry to be found in the books, papers, and articles that over the years have pronounced judgment on Congress for its many shortcomings, and after taking the institution to task for these deficiencies, the authors of these critical studies have usually reserved a portion of their lamentations for a list of reforms that they propose as correctives. Absent in these early reform proposals are any recommendations to cure excessive partisanship. The reason for that absence is obvious; it wasn't yet a problem. Indeed, the opposite case might well have posed greater problems for reformers, who tended, on the whole, to be political liberals: the conservative coalition that, since the late 1930s, had brought together southern Democrats and many northern Republicans to thwart liberal legislation.

What this suggests is that systemic national factors such as the internal composition of the political parties, the issues over which the parties compete, and overall demographics will determine the congressional reform agenda. Thus, we see reform recommendations that may be relevant at one period of congressional history but are time bound.

One of the pioneering books in this genre was the handiwork of Senator Joseph S. Clark, a liberal Pennsylvania Democrat who became one of the most relentless advocates of congressional reform. In 1965 he edited an anthology entitled *Congressional Reform: Problems and Prospects.*[1] Clark gathered everyone who was anyone into his reader, from eminent political scientists such as Richard Fenno, Ralph Huitt, and Donald Mathews to politicians such as Senator Jacob Javits (R-N.Y.) and House Rules Committee chairman, Representative Howard W. Smith (D-Va.) to experts on Congress from the world of journalism such as William S. White. The final chapter, "Coda: Making Congress Work," was written by Clark, who encapsulated the wisdom of the book's many contributors in four proposals for reform:

1. To change the party leadership structure so that within both parties and in both Houses, a majority will decide party policy and enforce party discipline.

2. To change the rules and procedures of both Houses so that a majority can act when it is ready to act.

3. To substitute cooperation for competition in the relations between the two Houses and between the Congress and the President, so that legislative recommendation [sic] of the President can be voted upon on their merits within a reasonable time after their submission to Congress.

4. To establish and enforce high ethical standards for members of Congress and its employees.[2]

It is easy to scoff at the quaintness of these recommendations, but they offer a valuable cautionary tale about efforts at structural reform in Congress, and it is this: the institutions of Congress are shaped by the larger political forces at a given time. To put it in the form of a simile, the best-tended fruit tree cannot survive climate change.

The climate in 1965 was influenced by several factors that were taken for granted by all of those involved in Senator Clark's worthy project. The first was a very clear bias on the part of most of the contributors in favor of presidential action. It should be recalled that these essays were written in the aftermath of the enactment of the Civil Rights Act of 1964, which from one perspective could be seen as a signal of congressional triumph, but it was President Lyndon B. Johnson, seeking to remove the blot of racism from the Democratic Party, who was its inspiration and driving force. The identification of civil rights progress with presidents—Democrats mostly—and associating obstruction with southern senators, also mostly Democrats, accounts for much of the pro-presidential bias.

Likewise, the push for strong, responsible party leadership was a brief for the growing influence of liberals in the two congressional Democratic caucuses over the forces of particularism defended by entrenched conservative committee chairmen. Clark and his collaborators could hardly have imagined the "Hastert Rule," an informal practice established in the late 1990s by then-speaker Dennis Hastert requiring that any bill brought up for a vote has the support of a majority of the majority party. If they could have foreseen it, they would likely have proclaimed it a triumphal culmination of responsible party government, had it not been promulgated by a Republican.

Although the passage of the Civil Rights Act and the subsequent election of 1964 signaled the onset of the conversion of the American South from Democratic to Republican, the North-South split within the Democratic Party, which then controlled all three branches of the federal government, influenced very strongly the tone of the Clark book and its reform proposals.

There is also an understandably strong anti-committee bias that emerges from the Clark group as well as a shot at the conservative coalition of Republicans and conservative Democrats that would today be seen as a healthy sign of bipartisanship.

In short, the differences in the overall political context between 1965 and 2013 not only suggest strongly how reform proposals can become stale and dated but also how the political conditions of the time set the boundaries of reform. Only the fusillade by Clark against the use of Rule XXII in the Senate, the cloture rule, has a contemporary ring to it, but the criticism then was aimed at its use in blocking civil rights legislation. We can only imagine what Clark would say about its frivolous use today.

Reform proposals in this early period tended to focus primarily on two abuses associated with Congress: seniority and venality. Accordingly, a popular book published in 1968 contained "ten modest proposals" for reform. All ten dealt with conflicts of interest and proposed banning members from practicing law while serving in Congress and barring members of the military reserves from serving on the armed services committees of the House and Senate. Interestingly, one of the 1968 reform proposals, that members of Congress disclose all assets and sources of income, was enacted only in 2012 with the passage of the Stock Act.[3]

Several years later Ralph Nader took his shot at Congress as part of the Ralph Nader Congress Project, an undertaking that produced a book entitled *Ruling Congress*. And here we have an example of reform proposals that are dated, but in a manner somewhat different from those of the Clark contributors, because they have been overtaken by events. Take, for example, some of the conclusions of the Nader report:

1. Closed-circuit television should be placed in the offices of all representatives and senators to broadcast floor proceedings, and

2. Computer terminals should be available in strategic places in the Capitol to facilitate immediate data retrieval concerning legislative scheduling, parliamentary rulings and so on.[4]

Been there, done that! Success in achieving reform goals certainly strengthens the case for promoting structural reform. The Nader group would probably be surprised that one of its reform proposals to attack the automatic seniority rule would be adopted as the result of the election in 1994 of the first Republican Congress in forty years.[5] The Nader report called for "automatic rotation of committee assignments," adding, "With a fluid committee membership, seniority would not likely govern the selection of chairmen because the hold Congressional leaders (senior members) exercise of junior members' careers would be weakened."[6] But the decision by the Republican conference in 1995 to term-limit chairs and ranking members, a step imitated by Senate Republicans, has not been an unalloyed blessing for the party or for the Senate.

Reform proposals have certainly not been uniformly quixotic or oblivious to the general context in which they have been made. Some reflect a kind of reform triumphalism; a report issued by the Center for Responsive Politics in 1986 reflects a kind of sweet complacency in concluding that "by the end of the 1970s, Congressional reformers had achieved many of their objectives. The Congress had become a more innovative and accountable institution. At the same time, it had recovered some of the policymaking authority it had given up to the other branches of government . . . In the past, younger members had to defer to more senior ones and the Congress was increasingly deferring to the executive on many issues. *Reform has changed that by redistributing power and providing opportunities at all levels.*"[7]

Summits and Grand Bargains

Until the 1990s, studies of Congress that included reform proposals rarely took note of the increase in partisanship and sought to offer correctives for it. Perhaps the most elaborate early examination of the rise of partisan polarization was by a former United States senator,

Fred R. Harris. He wrote that "each Senate party has become more internally cohesive on the issues. Party-line voting, especially on the most important votes, has increased. Party leaders and party conferences have become stronger, and the conferences have increasingly offered a needed mechanism for arching over Senate fragmentation."[8] This conclusion was written before the Republican takeover of the U.S. House of Representatives in 1995, an event pointed to by some as the origin of hyper-partisanship.

Harris quickly passes over the traditional sources of congressional dysfunction such as filibusters, noting, "A trend toward divided government has paralleled the increase in intraparty cohesion and unity in the Senate (and House), thus enlarging, rather than reducing, the possibilities of presidential-congressional conflict and government stalemate."[9] He follows this astute but apocalyptic observation by offering a solitary, and somewhat curious, reform proposal, suggesting that these forces "could be diminished by the institutionalization and greater use of the summit device to encourage cross-branch and cross-party cooperation on a range of issues."[10]

Harris's recommendation for bipartisan, bicameral, and bi-branch summits undoubtedly comes from the budget summit held over a period from May 15 to September 30, 1990, at the White House and at Andrews Air Force Base in Camp Springs, Maryland, just outside Washington. It was in the course of these meetings that President George H. W. Bush abandoned his "Read my lips, no new taxes" pledge made at the 1988 Republican National Convention by agreeing to raise $134 billion in new taxes. The compromise, designed to lower the deficit, was defeated in the House, and a government shutdown began. Ultimately, a Democratic budget was accepted with most of the details left to congressional committees.

The idea of summits to fashion "grand bargains" has had considerable appeal ever since 1983, when President Reagan and House Speaker Thomas P. "Tip" O'Neill agreed to a compromise to rescue the Social Security Trust Fund pursuant to the recommendation of a bipartisan commission headed by Alan Greenspan. The most recent effort to deal with intractable fiscal problems with a bipartisan summit came in the summer of 2011, when President Barack Obama and House Speaker John Boehner came close to a deal to extend the nation's borrowing limit.

The summit as a device to circumvent partisan polarization has a mixed record, but resort to such drastic measures is a confession of the failure of the institutions of government to resolve their differences in an orderly fashion. For one thing it bypasses the "regular order" of congressional committee hearings, markups, and committee reports. It elevates disputes into crises and shifts the debate away from congressional committees, where bipartisanship is common, and transfers it to the leadership level, where partisanship hits its highest pitch.

The 104th Congress and the Era of Internal Reform

No period in recent history has witnessed more sudden and sweeping changes than the 104th Congress (1995–97), when the Republicans became the majority in the House for the first time in forty years. It is important to note that although this period of congressional history is identified as one of heightened partisanship and polarization, as C. Lawrence Evans and Walter J. Oleszek noted in their 1997 book, *Congress under Fire,* "the nature of the agenda and the transition to Republican rule were partially responsible for these attributes [but] heightened congressional partisanship also characterized the last years of Democratic control." But, they added, "the Republican reorganization, which provided the procedural and structural underpinnings of the 104th Congress, served to reinforce and enhance these decision-making trends."[11]

While applauding some of the changes made by Speaker Newt Gingrich, including the application of workplace safety rules and employment laws to Congress and more consequential changes such as term limits on chairmanships, Evans and Oleszek clearly saw dangers in the centralization of power in the House leadership, which they identified as "the diminished quality and thoroughness of deliberation on Capitol Hill." They seemed less concerned about the Senate than they were about the House: "The [lower] chamber has been characterized by bitter partisanship, interpersonal acrimony, and a general lack of civility—all of which inhibit deliberation and collaboration across party lines."[12]

When it came to recommendations that might serve to dampen the fires of partisan polarization, Evans and Oleszek offered rather modest proposals. "One useful step," they wrote, "would be for lawmakers to educate their constituents more aggressively about the virtues of Congress's roles and the benefits of its 'messy' processes and procedures. Another worthwhile step might be for Congress to shed some of its individual and institutional workload so that lawmakers have more time for creative reflection and for concentration on effective policymaking."[13] These are worthy recommendations, but they appear, in light of current conditions, to point in a direction precisely opposite to where members are headed with their relentless fundraising, press handouts, press conferences, town meetings, and compressed legislative schedule.

Twenty-First Century Reform Proposals

By the beginning of the twenty-first century, party polarization in Congress was more or less taken for granted. Accordingly, in their 1999 study Kenneth R. Mayer and David T. Canon examined Congress's dysfunction largely in terms of the collective action problem.

They acknowledged that ideological polarization had intensified in the 1980s and 1990s and recognized that such correctives as holding retreats and civility weekends for members of Congress were "a step in the right direction" but not up to the task of reversing "a two-decade-long trend." They concluded that the decline in the norms of civility compounded the collective action problem.[14] They also offer the cautionary note that we should be careful about comparing the contemporary Congress with those of the "good old days," which, while perhaps more superficially genteel, were certainly no exemplars of the Homeric age.

The most consistent and celebrated critics of congressional dysfunction are two Washington-based political scientists, Thomas E. Mann and Norman J. Ornstein, who, through popular books and editorials, have both condemned the manner in which Congress operates and offered the most comprehensive proposals for reform. Beginning in 2006, Mann and Ornstein have taken on polarization along with many other problematic situations and practices in Congress and devoted the last eighteen pages of their first book, *The Broken Branch*, to reform under the Leninesque rubric "What Is to Be Done?" In it they realistically cautioned the reader that "no package of reforms will force lawmakers to develop a strong sense of institutional identity and loyalty, to strengthen an empty ethics process, to open up the policy process for serious deliberation, or to develop a new fealty to the regular order."[15]

Written before the Democratic re-conquest of Congress in 2006, Mann and Ornstein expressed the wistful hope that in the event that Democrats were to become the majority, "the political logic of divided government might well produce some reduction in partisan rancor and at least occasional cross-party agreement—although it would be difficult because any sizable Democratic gains come at least in part at the expense of Republican moderates." They suggested "convincing the national party committees to spread their resources to a larger number of contests, instead of concentrating as they do now on a few states, would help" to make more districts competitive, systemically and structurally, but they dismissed the argument that gerrymandering plays much of a role in political polarization in Congress while conceding that "redistricting makes a difficult situation considerably worse."[16]

In 2012 Mann and Ornstein returned to the topic of congressional dysfunction, but this time their attention was directly focused on polarization. Provocatively titled *It's Even Worse than It Looks,* the authors reserved special condemnation for the Republicans and in fact employed the term *asymmetric polarization:* "The center of gravity within the Republican Party has shifted sharply to the right. Its legendary moderate legislators in the House and Senate are virtually extinct. To be sure, a sizable number of the Republicans in Congress are center-right or right-center, rather than right-right. But the insurgent right wing regularly drowns them out."[17]

In an op-ed piece that accompanied the release of the book, Mann and Ornstein boiled down their reform proposals to four, after dismissing as unrealistic panaceas such correctives as a new third party, congressional term limits, a balanced budget, public financing of elections, and an updated version of the old London Blitz admonition "Keep Calm and Carry On." Instead, they placed their reform bets on (1) realistic campaign reform; (2) an independent commission for the decennial redistricting of the House; and (3) changing Senate Rule XXII to allow only one filibuster on any bill and compulsory voting.[18]

One of Mann's and Ornstein's reform recommendations was partially achieved in 2013 in the Senate by an agreement between Majority Leader Harry Reid and Minority Leader Mitch McConnell to modify Rule XXII to eliminate the filibuster on the motion to proceed providing that it permits each party votes on two amendments. In addition, the motion to send a bill to conference would be expedited, although the motion itself could still be filibustered.[19] The modification of Rule XXII does not answer all of Mann's and Ornstein's problems with the filibuster inasmuch as multiple veto points have been left in place. Campaign finance reform, while commendable, would do little to dampen partisan and ideological passions. On the other hand, the proposal to emulate the example of California and Iowa by establishing nonpartisan state redistricting commissions seems a worthy objective, but it would be a process that the states, individually, would have to adopt.

Three Modest Proposals

It would be charitable to say that past reform proposals have enjoyed a mixed record of success even when dealing with problems that are much more susceptible to structural reform than political polarization. System-wide hyper-partisanship is the product of factors of massive scope: demographics, social change in the United States over the past fifty years, vast changes in the economy, and the transformation of the media, among others. Against those engines of polarization, it is difficult merely to throw up one's hands and hope that, in the fullness of time, a gentler era will dawn. We can take some comfort in the cyclical nature of political forces, but that does not absolve us of the need to do a little constructive tinkering in those areas in which the quality of life in Congress might be strengthened and along with it, perhaps, we could see an improvement in the standing of Congress among the American people. Here, then, are three small things that might make a difference.

1. Repeal the 1974 Budget Act

Apart from the filibuster the amendment process for the budget resolution is the most partisan moment in Congress. The Senate's "vote-a-rama" is a pageant of message amendments designed to place colleagues of the opposing party on record in support of or in opposition to inflammatory amendments. The very process itself led Majority Leader Harry Reid to resist a budget for three years to protect his caucus from mischievous amendments. This outcome cannot have been the intention of the authors of the Budget Act.

While it would be important to retain the Congressional Budget Office, which the 1974 legislation also created, the entire budget process not only is dauntingly arcane and totally inaccessible even to the most attentive laity but promotes the most poisonous form of "gotcha" partisanship. A budget could be constructed perfectly well by the Joint Economic Committee, which could be endowed with legislative authority that is does not currently possess. Vesting the responsibility for the budget in a committee that is both bipartisan and bicameral would be applauded by reformers.

2. Abolish Term Limits for Chairman and Ranking Members

The ill-considered reform to remove term limits for top congressional leaders was a product of the "Gingrich revolution" in the House and was subsequently copied by Senate Republicans. It creates periodic havoc as senators and House members who have just mastered the fine points of their committee's jurisdiction are peremptorily ousted, along with their experienced staffs, and are replaced by personnel who face a steep and protracted learning curve.

The term limit is not only disruptive of the business of a committee; it also undermines bipartisanship because it supplants senior members who have over time developed cordial working relationships across party lines. It also results in staff shake-ups that impair, for a time at least, the functioning of the committee.

Such a disruption took place on the Senate Appropriations Committee in March 2013, when Senator Richard Shelby (R-Ala.) took over the ranking post from Senator Thad Cochran (R-Miss). Shelby fired five staff members who had worked for Cochran and one who had worked for outgoing senator Kay Bailey Hutchison (R-Tex.).[20]

Correcting this problem could be accomplished simply by changing Republican Party rules. Formal chamber rules need not be changed because the Democrats never adopted it as party policy.

3. Establish Bipartisan Committee Staffs

The Senate Select Intelligence Committee has used the practice of sharing a bipartisan staff to very good effect. This committee also houses its staff under a single roof, as does the much smaller Committee on Indian Affairs.

While it is true that the tone of bipartisanship (or lack of it) is set at the top by the chair and ranking minority member, closer personal staff relations across party lines would be facilitated by combining staff office arrangements.

Committees Nurture Bipartisanship

Two of the three reform recommendations proposed here apply to the committees of Congress on which bipartisanship maintains a reasonably strong foothold. Much of that has to with the fact that members of the committees tend to share external constituencies and enjoy expertise in common policy areas.

The committees are also more intimate settings—even the gigantic House committees—in which members get the opportunity to get acquainted with colleagues, going on congressional delegation trips, which, sadly, have been adversely affected by sequestration, and work together on drafting legislation.

In an era in which members feel that they are under a microscope trained on them by ideological interest groups, much of what happens in committees escapes the surveillance, and voting record scrutiny, of outside groups, which draw up their ratings based more on votes on final passage than on what happens in committee markups.

Restoring regular order and giving committees the opportunity to apply their experience and wisdom to legislation—rather than having it pass into the hands of party leaders where the partisanship is almost always more intense—is almost certain to decrease the likelihood of ideological warfare.

NOTES

1. Joseph S. Clark, ed., *Congressional Reform: Problems and Prospects* (New York: Thomas Y. Crowell, 1965).

2. Clark, *Congressional Reform*, 346.

3. Drew Pearson and Jack Anderson, *The Case against Congress: A Compelling Indictment of Corruption on Capitol Hill* (New York: Simon and Schuster, 1968), 451.

4. Ralph Nader, *Ruling Congress* (New York: Penguin Books, 1975), 207.

5. Nader, *Ruling Congress*, 208.

6. Nader, *Ruling Congress*, 208.

7. Peter Lindstrom, *Congressional Operations: Not for the Short Winded: Congressional Reform, 1961–1986* (Washington, D.C.: Center for Responsive Politics, 1986), 49; emphasis added.

8. Fred R. Harris, *Deadlock or Decision: The U.S. Senate and the Rise of National Politics* (New York: Oxford University Press, 1993), 271.

9. Harris, *Deadline or Decision*.

10. Harris, *Deadline or Decision*.

11. C. Lawrence Evans and Walter J. Oleszek, *Congress under Fire: Reform Politics and the Republican Majority* (Boston: Houghton Mifflin, 1997), 176–77.

12. Evans and Oleszek, *Congress under Fire*.

13. Evans and Oleszek, *Congress under Fire*, 179.

14. Kenneth R. Mayer and David T. Canon, *The Dysfunctional Congress? The Individual Roots of an Institutional Dilemma* (Boulder: Westview Press, 1999), 86.

15. See Thomas E. Mann and Norman J. Ornstein, *The Broken Branch: How Congress is Failing America and How to Get It Back on Track* (New York: Oxford University Press, 2006), 231.

16. Mann and Ornstein, *Broken Branch*, 227, 230–31.

17. Thomas E. Mann and Norman J. Ornstein, *It's Even Worse than It Looks: How the American Constitutional System Collided with the New Politics of Extremism* (New York: Basic Books, 2012), 51–52.

18. Norman J. Ornstein and Thomas E. Mann, "Want to End Partisan Politics? Here's What Won't Work—and What Will," *Washington Post,* May 17, 2012.

19. Alexander Bolton, "Reid and McConnell Reach Tentative Deal to Change Filibuster Rules," *Hill,* January 24, 2013; and Man Raju, "Reid, McConnell Reach Senate Filibuster Deal," *Politico,* January 24, 2013.

20. Austin Wright and Jonathan Allen, "Richard Shelby Sacks Six Appropriations Aides," *Politico,* March 25, 2013.

Voices of Former Members of Congress

Former Representative Mickey Edwards (R-Okla.): We have gotten so far away from the regular order—which was where people who had knowledge of the issues and who had a special interest in advancing, whether it's agricultural issues or environmental issues, or whatever—we'd sit down and work it out.

Today it tends to be coming from the top down, where it's a messaging issue. It's more about how you frame the message in order to win the next election than it is to deal with the legislative problem that you've got. I love the guys who are sitting up here who took roles as leaders, and they considered themselves legislative leaders. I think more and more the people today who are in leadership positions in the House and Senate see themselves as party leaders, and they, too, have lost the idea of how do we get something done so that you can keep the water pure and keep the bridges from collapsing—things like that—that are the responsibilities of Congress.

A lot of it is that even in the leadership ranks, there's been a diminishing idea of what it means when you take the oath of office. It doesn't mean how can you position your party to win the next election.

Former Senator Blanche Lincoln (D-Ark.): One of the things that's critically important that's missing on Capitol Hill, I think, today is time. It's time for members to be able to grow the respect and the relationships that they need to have the respect for one another, so that they can do what it is that they need to do, and that is come together and find the center ground, find where you agree, and then move from that.

I do agree that the parties have created this issue of leadership as meaning control. Leadership doesn't mean control. I'm sitting next to some leaders here who weren't in there to control. Leadership means creating an environment where people feel comfortable coming to the table and offering their ideas. They feel respected by other people whom they're working with. That's what real leadership means. It means really bringing together people in an environment where they feel comfortable looking for the answers.

I think that's a really critical thing for us to think about in terms of leadership, whether it's leadership in the Congress, leadership in the parties. I think the key word in there is *respect*. The way that you respect one another is by getting to know them, and you cannot get to know people if you do not spend time with them.

The idea of maybe once a month doing a caucus together, as opposed to going off into your separate rooms—the Democrats in one and the Republicans in another. . . . When I first came [to the Senate], my predecessor, Dale Bumpers [D-Ark.], who spent four terms in the United States Senate, said to me, he said: "I know that you'll do a great job. I'm really proud of you. I only wish you could know the Senate that I knew." He said, "I'm more liberal than you are, but my best friends, some of my best friends were Republicans." And he said: "It wasn't because we agreed on the policy. It was because we were friends. We raised our kids together. We had to go to those awful band concerts together. We had to do the kind of things that create relationships." He kept encouraging me to travel on the CODELs [congressional delegation overseas fact-finding trips]. He said, "You really get to know your colleagues."

That wasn't an option for me. I was very, very young. Looking back, naïveté was my greatest asset, I think. I didn't know I wasn't supposed to be here.

But, I had young children. My dad was in failing health. There were just many other things that I had to do that I did not want to wake up one day and regret that I hadn't been there for them, but I made it an effort to make sure that I went to every one of those spouse dinners. And I made Steve Lincoln come, and I made us sit at a table with somebody that we did not know. He said, "Why are we sitting with these people?" I said: "Because we don't know them, and we need to know them. These are people who I work with who are making a difference in this world, and we need to know who they are."

It was hysterical. I will never forget the first time I sat next to [former senator] Judd Gregg [R-N.H.] and his wife. All of a sudden, we walked out of there, and Judd looked at me, and he said, "Am I buying your piano?" I said, "Well, your wife and I have been talking about this." Something that never would have happened had we not gotten to know one another and gotten to be better friends, and even though we may have disagreed, we respected one another, enough to try to find that common ground.

③

The Challenge of Bipartisanship
A Historical Perspective

Frances E. Lee

The problems Congress faces today in getting bipartisan agreement are new to postwar American government. There should be no doubt that it is much harder for politicians to work across party lines today than it was in the 1950s, 1960s, and 1970s. It is even harder than it was in the 1980s and 1990s. Party has always been the single best predictor of how members of Congress will vote. But conflict between the parties has become far more rigid and pervasive. The factors that have brought about this polarization are large-scale, long-term trends that are deeply rooted in the incentives of politicians. They will not be amenable to simple or quick institutional or procedural fixes.

The rise of party conflict in Congress can be seen with a variety of measures. First, one can turn to measures of party loyalty—the percentage of the time members vote with their parties on issues that divide a majority of one party from a majority of the other.[1] Figures 1 and 2 display average Republican and Democratic Party loyalty among House and Senate members between 1956 and 2010. In the 1950s, 1960s, and 1970s the typical senator voted with his or her party on controversial issues just over 60 percent of the time; in the 1980s it was just over 70 percent of the time; and in the 1990s it was just over 80 percent of the time. Since 2000 senators have voted with their parties on average above 87 percent of the time. The story is the same in the House.

Note the parallel polarization in the House and Senate, even though those institutions are very different from one another. House

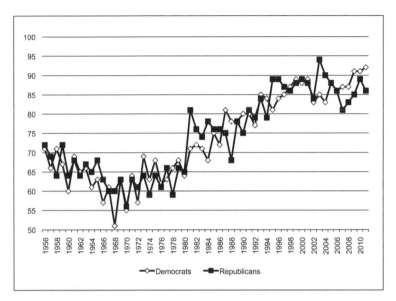

Fig. 1. Party Loyalty in the U.S. Senate, 1956–2010, by Percentage

Source: Emily Ethridge, "2011 Vote Studies: Party Unity," *CQ Weekly,* January 15, 2012, 111–16.

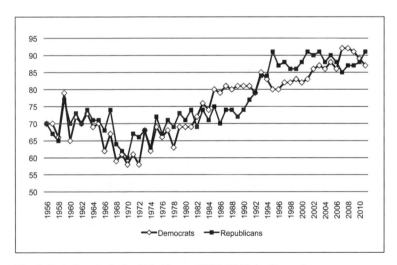

Fig. 2. Party Loyalty in the U.S. House, 1956–2010, by Percentage

Source: Emily Ethridge, "2011 Vote Studies: Party Unity," *CQ Weekly,* January 15, 2012, 111–16.

constituencies can and are gerrymandered for many reasons, and this affects which party can win any given seat. But the Senate is never re-districted or gerrymandered, and it has seen a similar level of height-ened party conflict as the House.

A second way of looking at party polarization is to gauge the num-ber of moderates in Congress.[2] By "moderates," we mean lawmakers who vote with the opposing party on controversial issues with some frequency.[3] According to this measure, as shown in figure 3, more than half of all lawmakers in both the House and Senate were mod-erate in the 1950s. Around 40 percent were moderates through the 1960s and 1970s. But the share of moderates has been declining pre-cipitously since the early 1980s. In the 112th Congress moderates con-stituted 12 percent of the Senate and a mere 6 percent of the House.

Conflict always slows Congress down, partisan conflict most of all. And as partisan conflict has spread to a greater number of issues, the

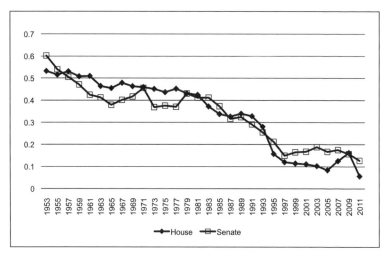

Fig. 3. Proportion of Moderate Legislators in Congress, 1951–2011, by Percentage

Source: Keith Poole and Howard Rosenthal, "The Polarization of the Congressional Parties," Voteview.com, http://voteview.com/political_polarization.asp (accessed January 31, 2013).

institution has become progressively more bogged down. As a consequence, the 112th Congress accomplished almost nothing. As a gauge of legislative productivity, figure 4 shows the total number of public laws passed in each Congress since 1951. With the passage of only 240 laws, the 112th Congress is the least productive of the whole time series. As partisanship has increased in Congress, there has been a long trend toward lower productivity by this measure. But productivity in the 112th Congress was nearly half of the baseline established after 1994. About twice as many laws were cleared during George W. Bush's difficult two years of divided government following the 2006 midterms.

It may not be surprising that a divided Congress in which Democrats have a Senate majority and Republicans control the House

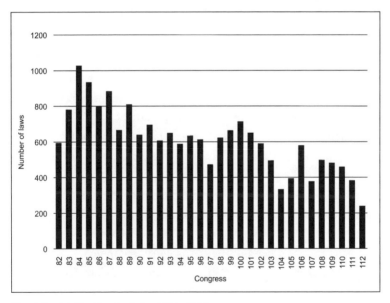

Fig. 4. Legislative Productivity, 1951–2012

Source: Norman J. Ornstein, Thomas E. Mann, and Michael J. Malbin, *Vital Statistics on Congress, 2008* (Washington, D.C.: Brookings Institution, 2008); data on the most recent congresses from the Library of Congress–thomas, http://thomas.loc.gov/home/thomas.php.

failed to compromise on the most controversial issues dividing the two parties: taxes and spending. But it has been enormously hard for the Congress to act on anything, even on previously low-profile, bipartisan issues.

Recently Congress has been unable to pass significant legislation on transportation infrastructure (roads, bridges, airports). The 112th Congress couldn't even pass a farm bill—Congress hadn't had as much trouble with a farm bill in fifty years. The U.S. Postal Service defaulted on its obligations in the summer of 2013, but Congress was unable to act. Increasingly, it seems that almost all issues are being realigned along the main partisan cleavage, making it extraordinarily difficult for the Congress to act and for presidents to lead Congress.

Roots of Party Conflict
Constituency Changes

Changes in congressional constituencies—which have developed over decades—have created an institution in which there are far fewer cross-pressured members. Over the past thirty years voters have become more consistently partisan in their voting behavior. They don't split their tickets to nearly the same extent as in the past. Voters today are much more likely to cast ballots for candidates of the same party across different political offices.[4] Figure 5 displays the percentage of voters splitting their tickets in national elections since 1952. By the first decade of the twenty-first century voters were as consistent in preferring the same party's candidates across different national offices as they had been in the 1950s. Very few members represent states or districts that voted for the opposing party's presidential candidate. In 2012 only around 11 percent of districts went one way in voting for the House and the other in voting for the president.

Another key form of constituency change has been the regional realignment of the parties. As shown in figure 6, the South went from

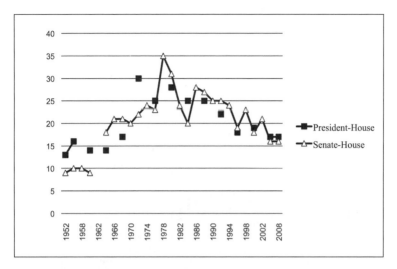

Fig. 5. Split Ticket Voting, 1952–2008, by Percentage

Source: Harold W. Stanley and Richard G. Niemi, eds., *Vital Statistics on American Politics,* 2011–2012 (Washington, D.C.: CQ Press, 2011), http://library.cqpress.com/vsap/vsap11_ tab3-20, table 3-10.

being solidly Democratic in the 1950s and 1960s and heavily Democratic in the 1970s to being two-party competitive in the 1980s and, since the 1990s, Republican dominated.

Partisan change in the South is important for the way it has transformed the political incentives of members. A large share of the moderates in postwar congresses were these southern Democrats. They were politicians who needed for their political survival to maintain some political distance from the national Democratic Party. This meant that it was strongly in their political interests to look for ways to work across party lines and to stake out issue positions that differentiated them from the national Democratic Party. Republicans elected from the South today do not need or seek any cross-party alliances in order to improve their political credibility with constituents. In fact, if they create a problem for their national parties, it's mainly by their unwillingness to work across party lines.

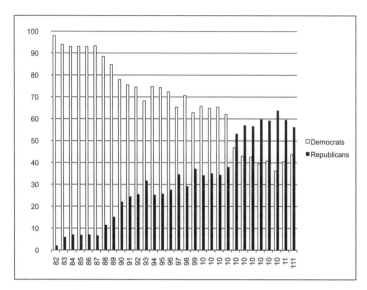

Fig. 6. Party Affiliation of House Members from the South, 1951–2010, by Percentage

Source: Data collected by author.

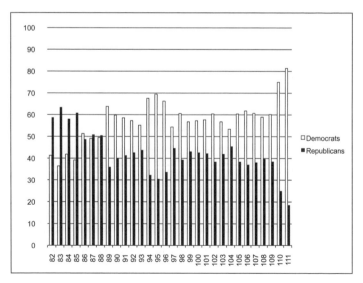

Fig. 7. Party Affiliation of House Members from the Northeast, 1951–2010, by Percentage

Source: Data collected by author.

Figure 7 shows that there is a parallel development with the Northeast, which went from being a Republican region in the 1950s to a two-party competitive region in the 1960s to a heavily Democratic region today. Northeastern Republicans had been the Republican equivalent of southern Democrats. By pursuing cross-party alliances, they differentiated themselves from the mainstream of the Republican Party. The region first realigned after the 1964 elections, when presidential candidate Barry Goldwater's forces won control of the Republican Party. It has become progressively more Democratic ever since. All in all the contemporary political environment provides fewer incentives for members of Congress to look for any ways to obscure or downplay their party affiliations to voters.

Competition for Party Control of Institutions

One of the most striking things about the American political system today is its ferocious competitiveness. One can see this enhanced competition in a variety of ways. For many years after 1932, Democrats were viewed as the nation's natural majority party in Congress. The 1980 elections destabilized this conventional wisdom. The 1994 elections put the whole question permanently to rest. There is no majority party in American politics today.

The two parties are at near parity in terms of voter support in the country. Democrats had a large advantage over Republicans for many decades, in that far more Americans identified as Democrats than as Republicans. But since the 1980s the two parties have gradually converged in terms of their share of the electorate.

Recent decades have seen narrow congressional majorities. For the decade of the 1930s Democrats had two-to-one margins over Republicans. There was a brief period of party competition in the 1940s and 1950s. But by 1960 the Congress stood again at two-to-one Democratic margins, and big Democratic majorities held through the 1970s.

Since 1980 no party has had a majority like those enjoyed by the Democrats during most of the post–New Deal period. Between 1980 and 2007 there have been six switches of party control of the Senate. Although Democrats held their majorities longer in the House than in the Senate, beginning in 1994, the party balance in the House has been extremely tight.

Today there is continuous speculation about what it will take to return the minority party to the majority. Competition is a powerful spur to party organization. Their common stake in winning control of the institution gives members powerful incentives to cooperate with their fellow partisans.

In such an environment "every vote is about the next election," observed Senator Lindsey Graham (R-S.C.).[5] The result is the rise of message politics.[6] More and more votes in Congress are staged for the purpose of highlighting the differences between the two parties. Many votes are taken on bills that no one has any illusion will become law. Members are quite frank about that. The purpose of a partisan message vote is to put a politically attractive idea before the public and then to demonstrate that it cannot pass given the current party composition of national institutions. Message votes are designed to fail. They're not serious efforts to legislate. The goal is communication, not lawmaking. Public relations takes up enormous amounts of time in the contemporary Congress.

Party Institutions

One way to track power in Congress is to look at staff levels. There has been an enormous amount of growth in the congressional party organizations. Since the late 1970s there has been a more than 300 percent increase in the number of staff working for Senate party leaders (fig. 8). Meanwhile, committee staff levels have stayed flat. As late as 1981, neither party had much by way of internal party organization.

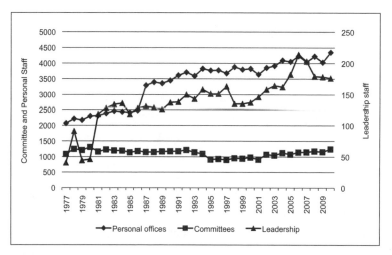

Fig. 8. Senate Staff Levels, 1977–2010

Source: R. Eric Peterson, Parker H. Reynolds, and Amber Hope Wilhelm, *House of Representatives and Senate Staff Levels in Member, Committee, Leadership, and Other Offices, 1977–2010,* CRS Report for Congress, R41366 (Washington, D.C.: Congressional Research Service, August 10, 2010).

Senate Democrats seldom met together in the same room.[7] Now both parties have elaborate party organizations. There are so many meetings of party groups that members rarely meet or socialize with members of the opposition party.[8]

A lot of important legislation that passes today has never even received committee consideration. On high-profile matters, as journalist David Weigel aptly put it, the deals rocket from the secret talks straight to the House and Senate floor.[9]

Effects on Legislation

The rules and procedures of the House of Representatives permit majority rule.[10] A House majority party that can hold its ranks together can accomplish its legislative program. The majority party uses its control over the agenda to ensure that legislation is considered under favorable conditions, frequently denying the minority party the opportunity to participate or offer amendments that have the potential to embarrass or undermine the majority's coalition. The House of Representatives is usually able to cope with increased party conflict via simple majority rule. Yet the minority party's refusal en masse to vote in favor of the majority's initiatives can place a lot of pressure on a party that holds only a narrow majority. To succeed in legislating, such leaders must win nearly universal party loyalty, including from their most marginal members. On some occasions this pressure is too much for a majority party to withstand. Internal defections may render a House majority unable to legislate without some cross-party support.

Increased party unity has created even more serious obstacles for successful legislating in the Senate.[11] Unlike the House of Representatives, where a simple majority is sufficient to force a measure to a vote, Senate rules require a supermajority to obtain "cloture," meaning an end to debate. The minority party has come to exploit extended debate to obstruct much of the majority party's legislative agenda. Senate minority parties routinely orchestrate a coordinated filibuster, usually manifested as bloc voting against cloture. Since the 1990s the filibuster has emerged, in effect, as a minority party veto on legislation. The party polarization that has streamlined House procedures has led to rampant obstructionism in the Senate.

The consequences of these changes for policy making create very real tendencies toward gridlock. It is very difficult for Congress to do anything at all, except when facing down an immediate crisis. Under unified government today's level of party conflict means that the majority party has to try to govern alone, without bipartisan support—a difficult proposition. But it's even more difficult to get partisan legislation through the Senate. Under divided government party conflict also means very limited progress.

In such an environment there is little room for policy entrepreneurship outside the parties. By way of contrast, one might think back to Senator Warren Rudman, a New Hampshire Republican, a centrist, a legislative dealmaker who had the ability to make things happen outside party lines and around his party leadership. One of Rudman's most famous efforts along these lines was the Gramm-Rudman-Hollings agreement of 1985. This legislation was very similar to the debt ceiling agreement of 2011: either reduce the deficit, or automatic cuts would be imposed. It was even passed as a condition of raising the debt ceiling, much to the annoyance of President Reagan.[12] Compare Rudman's efforts with those of the Gang of Six or the Gang of Eight in the Senate during the 112th Congress, which worked to reach a grand bargain. The group met continuously for more than a year, until the fall just before the 2012 elections. These were extended meetings, representing a significant effort on the part of all participants, undertaken at some political risk. The result: nothing.

All the key deals in recent congresses have been brokered through leadership offices. There seems to be little room for working outside or around the parties now. The bottom line is that we shouldn't have any illusions about how profoundly difficult it is to make policy in today's circumstances. Nor should we have any illusions about just how difficult it will be to reverse the long-term transformations that have given rise to these deep and pervasive partisan conflicts.

NOTES

1. Emily Ethridge, "2011 Vote Studies: Party Unity," *CQ Weekly,* January 15, 2012, 111–16.

2. For more detail on the measurement, see Nolan McCarty, Keith T. Poole, and Howard Rosenthal, *Polarized America: The Dance of Ideology and Unequal Riches* (Cambridge: MIT Press, 2006). Data downloaded from Poole and Rosenthal's website, Vote view.com, hosted by the Department of Political Science at the University of Georgia.

3. McCarty, Poole, and Rosenthal, *Polarized America*.

4. Barry C. Burden and David C. Kimball, *Why Americans Split Their Tickets: Campaigns, Competition, and Divided Government* (Ann Arbor: University of Michigan Press, 2002).

5. Quoted in Carl Hulse, "As Aisle Gets Wider, Arms Get Shorter," *New York Times*, December 28, 2009.

6. Frances E. Lee, "Making Laws and Making Points: Senate Governance in an Era of Uncertain Majorities," *Forum* 9, no. 4 (2011): article 3.

7. Rob Liberatore, "Who Knew Lunches Would Lead to Gridlock?" *Politico*, November 20, 2008, www.politico.com/news/stories/1108/15792.html (accessed on September 19, 2013).

8. Ron Fournier, "In Congress, Compromise Is a 4-Letter Word," *National Journal*, May 30, 2013, www.nationaljournal.com/politics/in-congress-compromise-is-a-4-letter-word-20130117 (accessed on September 19, 2013).

9. David Weigel, "Remembering the Republican 'Pledge to America,'" *Weigel: Reporting on Politics and Policy* blog, *Slate Magazine*, January 2, 2013, www.slate.com/blogs/weigel/2013/01/02/_we_will_fight_efforts_to_use_a_national_crisis_for_political_gain_remembering.html (accessed on September 19, 2013).

10. Walter J. Oleszek, *Congressional Procedures and the Policy Process*, 7th ed. (Washington, D.C.: CQ Press, 2007).

11. Barbara Sinclair, *Unorthodox Lawmaking: New Legislative Processes in the U.S. Congress*, 4th ed. (Washington, D.C.: CQ Press, 2012).

12. Interview with Warren B. Rudman, "Slaying the Dragon of Debt: Fiscal Politics and Policy from the 1970s to the Present," Regional Oral History Office, Bancroft Library, University of California–Berkeley, interviews conducted in 2010 by Patrick Sharma and Martin Meeker, http://digitalassets.lib.berkeley.edu/roho/ucb/text/rudman_warren.pdf (accessed on September 19, 2013).

Voices of Former Members
of Congress

Former Senator Byron Dorgan (D-N.Dak.): I think there's been a culture change in the Congress in the way it works. There's no question about that, and the question is what has caused that and what can be done to remedy it.

When I showed up [in the Senate in 1992], you were rewarded for compromise and punished for obstruction. By that I mean if you were a senator or a congressman and you spent most of your time trying to find compromises and pass legislation, generally speaking, you were rewarded in your caucus, you were rewarded by your constituents. And if you spent most of your time being a real pain and deciding I'm going to be a set of human brake pads, I'm going to stop everything to the extent I can, you were largely punished by your caucus and by your constituents.

Now I think it's safe to say that obstructionism is largely rewarded, and compromise is punished. This will be controversial, so bear with me for a moment. I think since the late 1980s, [because of deregulation by the Federal Communications Commission], the growth of talk radio and cable television has meant the following: You have a playing floor, with the politicians on the playing floor in the U.S. Congress. Then you have the bleacher section, and in recent decades that bleacher section now has microphones, and some microphones extend to fifteen and twenty million people a day. So they watch the floor, that playing floor, and they say: "Oh, look at that person. That person is compromising and therefore not standing up for their principles. Shame on that person. Shame on them." You pay a very significant price in Congress if you are compromising these days because the master narrative is that compromise means that you don't stand for your principles. That has had a profound impact on politics in this town.

It's controversial because when you talk about that, somebody says, "Well, you're blaming this or that." I think there need to be joint caucuses. In almost every enterprise in life, you would try to figure out with the people you're with what's the strategy, what do we need to get done, and how do we do it. That's not the case in Congress these days.

The question is what's the strategy for our caucus, not for our country. To use a metaphor of baseball, it's very much like a baseball game where you have two dugouts, and you never see people go back and forth between the dugouts at all. There's their team, and there's our team. There's Republicans and Democrats. Now, what we do we want? We want the other side to lose. That didn't exist decades ago.

Decades ago, ranking members and chairmen and the men and women who served there by and large would get together and decide what do we have to do for the country, what deadlines do we have to meet, how are we going to meet them, and they ran their caucuses.

Leadership is much more difficult now, if not impossible, when you're trying to deal with cable television and talk radio and a whole series of things back home in a constituency that says, "You know what, we're going to tune in to listen to those things on the radio and television, and only that which reinforces our existing belief," and they're going to tell us whether our person is one of those people who is not standing for principles but in fact is compromising. We call it a four-letter word, and we hate four-letter words, and we're going to punish those who are compromisers.

This can be remedied, but it's hard, and the country desperately needs leadership and understanding that compromise is the lubrication of democracy. It is the only way democracy can possibly work. When you believe something and I believe something very different, we come together in good fellowship and decide here is where we can meet in the middle to help advance the country's interest.

Congress and Electoral Reform in the Early Twenty-First Century

Brian L. Fife

According to the American people, there is something profoundly wrong with the most democratic institution of government, the Congress of the United States. Gallup pollsters provide the data to substantiate this claim. Since April 1974 American adults have been asked, "Do you approve or disapprove of the way Congress is handling its job?"[1] Approval of Congress has averaged 34 percent across more than 230 polls since the Watergate era.[2] Congress's highest approval rating occurred in October 2001, a month after the terrorist attacks in New York City and Washington, D.C. (84 percent). But it has been below 40 percent since early 2005, and it has been below 20 percent every month since June 2011, except for once in October 2012, when approval registered at 21 percent. Record low approval ratings were garnered twice in 2012 (10 percent).[3] Clearly, though Congress as an institution has not typically been exceedingly popular in terms of job performance, what is happening recently in the arena of public opinion is absolutely abysmal. A healthy republic must have a functional legislative body; otherwise, rampant cynicism, distrust, frustration, and downright anger pervade society and culture in a profound manner.

There is documented consensus that Congress as an institution can and must be improved. The American people will not witness such a transformation until members of Congress reform the manner in which the people of the United States select them in the first place. Winning elections is commendable, for service in the U.S. Congress is contingent upon it in most, but not all, circumstances. Yet a flawed electoral process has a detrimental effect on the ability of members to engage in public policy making. Fundamentally, service in Congress is not about polling, fund-raising, and the constant campaign. The measure of an effective legislator is a person who gets things done. In order to pass legislation in a republic with separation of powers and checks and balances, lawmakers must be adept at the art of political compromise. If the electoral methodology compromises the ability of lawmakers to be effective, then reform measures can substantively enhance the conditions for effective public policy making. Even more important, democratic electoral reform has long been a part of the American tradition, and the current members of Congress must not ignore and fail to do their duty to ensure that the electoral process is as facilitative as possible. With this in mind, I would like to offer a number of proposals designed not only to make Congress a more effective public policy–making institution but simultaneously to enhance democracy in America as well.

Congress's Own Rich History in Electoral Reform

Many democratic electoral changes have been passed by members of Congress in U.S. history. Among some of the more notable changes include the passage of the Fifteenth Amendment (1870), the Seventeenth Amendment (1913), the Nineteenth Amendment (1920), the Twenty-Fourth Amendment (1964), the Voting Rights Act (1965), the Twenty-Sixth Amendment (1971), and the National Voter Registration Act (1993).[4] State reform efforts have also been prominent in American history, particularly during the Progressive Era, with the advent of the direct primary and the evolution of the Australian ballot, the initiative, referendum, and recall.[5]

Heeding lessons from history is essential to today's legislator who wishes to contribute to the democratic tradition in the United States.

Reforming electoral procedures in the United States has been a recurring theme ever since the first formal session of Congress in 1789. History is replete with such cases in two substantive ways. First, efforts to promote electoral fairness and the democratic ethos do not always succeed, especially in short-term circumstances. Well-intended reformers often meet with failure, at least initially, in their quest to enhance popular sovereignty. The successful reformer is the legislator who remains patient and does not capitulate to his or her opponents. Second, reforming electoral procedures is a constant work in progress in an imperfect system. Human enterprises are flawed by definition and always fraught with error; the key to electoral reform is to constantly make the process more democratic in the world's oldest functioning democracy.

The Role of Congress in Federal Elections
under the Constitution

At the Philadelphia convention in 1787, the framers of the Constitution determined that voting in the United States would be an exercise in federalism, in which certain powers were given to Congress and other powers were left for the state governments. Under Article I, Section 4, "the Times, Places, and Manner of holding Elections for Senators and Representatives, shall be prescribed in each State by the Legislature thereof; but the Congress may at any time by Law make or alter such Regulations." Thus, the framers allowed state legislators to essentially create the rules of governing their own elections, but members of Congress had the authority to intervene when they deemed necessary. One of the more significant interventions by Congress occurred in 1845, when its members established a national Election Day for the first time in U.S. history.[6] Previously, states were permitted to conduct their presidential elections any time during a thirty-four-day period (before the first Wednesday in December) pursuant to a law passed by congressional members on March 1, 1792.[7] In 1875 members of Congress determined that electing U.S. representatives on Election Day every even-numbered year would be prudent, and this idea was applied to U.S. senators as well in 1914 in the aftermath of the passage of the Seventeenth Amendment.[8]

The simple reality is that members of Congress have intervened in American election law when state officials failed to meet their constitutional duties. Regarding selecting electors in presidential elections, it was clear that the outcomes in some states influenced the vote in the others, so Congress changed its own law to make the electoral process more fair and equitable. When state officials denied the right to vote to certain classes of citizens, typically the result of a lengthy civil rights struggle, our elected leaders responded because they had a duty to do so. That duty—to provide citizens with equal access to the ballot box—has not withered away and become moot in today's society. In fact, there are a number of unhealthy indicators in the American Republic that need to be addressed in a forthright manner because delay and neglect have been the norm for far too long. By way of consideration for the members of Congress, I propose a series of reforms that, taken collectively, will enhance the electoral process in the United States without compromising its integrity.

Reform Proposal #1:
Reform Stringent Voter Registration Laws

Regardless of one's beliefs about American federalism, it is important to heed the sage counsel of both Alexander Hamilton and James Madison when they drafted *The Federalist Papers* after the Constitution was written in 1787. Although they would later part ways politically, Hamilton, in *The Federalist* No. 28, and Madison, in *The*

Federalist No. 46, reminded citizens that the fundamental reality in a republican form of government is that the ultimate sovereigns in the United States are the people. Government officials, at either the national or subnational levels, are nothing more than trustees of the people.[9] Conflicts over federalism should be subordinate to the more substantive objective of enhancing democracy and attending to the collective interests of the people. In terms of federal elections, how can the process be reformed so as to promote the cause of democracy in the United States?

Many state officials have a record of not making voting facilitative for the citizens. When it comes to voter registration, the optimum scenario would be to replicate the North Dakota model. There all citizens become eligible to vote when they reach their eighteenth birthday. The burden of proof for registration is on the state and not on the individual. Most democracies use this methodology because it actually encourages people to participate in the electoral process. Members of Congress could intervene on behalf of the people. Too many state laws are antiquated on this matter because election officials are still operating on the precedent established in *Dunn v. Blumstein* (1972).[10] Based on the computer technology of the early 1970s, the justices in that case determined that states could mandate that citizens be compelled to register to vote up to thirty days before an election.[11] Today people can secure thousands of dollars in credit in minutes, but residents in thirty-one states have to register between twenty-one to thirty days in advance of an election.[12] Otherwise, such people effectively waive their right to vote until the next election. A second option to encourage more citizen participation at the ballot box would be to implement Election Day registration across the nation. Election Day registration is currently utilized in nine states (Colo., Idaho, Iowa, Maine, Minn., Mont., N.H., Wis., and Wyo.) plus the District of Columbia. In addition, another two states, California and Connecticut, have enacted legislation establishing same-day registration but have not yet implemented it. Two other states, North Carolina and Ohio, allow voters to register and cast a vote during a state-prescribed early voting period. Finally, in 2016 Maryland will also allow residents to register and vote on the same day during the early voting period but not on Election Day itself. In Election Day or same-day registration states, average voter turnout rates are ten to twelve percentage points higher than the national average.[13]

Voting is a preeminent right in a democracy. As such, citizens of the United States should be treated in an equitable and undifferentiated manner. Access to the ballot should be universal; computer technology is much too sophisticated today to justify a waiting period of up to thirty days before an election. In the wisdom of the framers of the Constitution, public servants in Congress can intervene in state election law at any time they find it prudent to do so. On the matter of voter registration in many states, the debate needs to shift away from federalism to substance. Is it reasonable to deter voting through the reliance of antiquated laws? Where equitable conditions do not exist across the country, members of Congress have a responsibility to be the intervener on behalf of the people.

On January 23, 2013, Representative John Lewis (D-Ga.) proposed the Voter Empowerment Act of 2013 in the House of Representatives.[14] Senator Kirsten Gillibrand (D-N.Y.) proposed this bill in the Senate on the same day.[15] According to officials at the Brennan Center for Justice, this legislation would provide a comprehensive approach to electoral reform and would result in the maximization of technology in voting at the present time.[16] Increasing voter participation in the United States while simultaneously protecting the integrity of the electoral system are time-honored objectives to reformers, and members of today's Congress have the opportunity to enhance the electoral system now and should do so without further delay.

Reform Proposal #2:
Reform Laws Regarding Felons

According to officials at the Brennan Center for Justice, about 6 million U.S. citizens cannot vote because of a past criminal conviction. Approximately 4.4 million of these Americans live, work, and raise families in communities but are unable to vote. Many of the state laws regarding felons and the franchise are artifacts of a disconcerting racial history, and they have a disparate impact on minorities. Across the United States 13 percent of all African American men have lost their right to vote, a rate that is seven times the national average for all citizens of voting age.[17]

Felony voting rights vary considerably by state. Policies governing felons and the franchise can be placed into six broad categories: permanent disenfranchisement for all people with felony convictions (Fla., Iowa, Ky., and Va.); permanent disenfranchisement for at least some people with felony convictions (Ala., Ariz., Del., Miss., Nev., Tenn., and Wyo.); voting rights restored upon completion of sentence, including prison, parole, and probation (Alaska, Ark., Ga., Idaho, Kans., La., Md., Minn., Mo., Neb., N.J., N.Mex., N.C., Okla., S.C., Tex., Wash., W.Va., and Wis.); voting rights restored automatically after release from prison and discharge from parole (Calif., Colo., Conn., N.Y., and S.Dak.); voting rights restored automatically after release from prison (D.C., Hawaii, Ill., Ind., Mass., Mich., Mont., N.H., N.Dak., Ohio, Ore., Pa., R.I., and Utah); and no disenfranchisement for people with felony convictions (Maine and Vt.).[18] A broad gamut exists in current state laws, for a citizen convicted of a felony in Maine or Vermont can cast an absentee ballot from jail while serving his or her sentence; if that person commits the same crime in Florida, Iowa, Kentucky, or Virginia, he or she may never vote again unless voting rights are restored by official state action.[19]

In 2011 Representative John Conyers (D-Mich.) introduced the Democracy Restoration Act of 2011 in the House.[20] Later that year

Senator Benjamin Cardin (D-Md.) replicated this move in the Senate.[21] The measure has not been passed. Currently, fifteen states and the District of Columbia have laws that restore voting rights when individuals are released from prison; thirty-five states have statutes that continue to restrict the franchise to those who are no longer incarcerated. This practice is not reasonable, does not serve a compelling state interest, and does not provide citizens with equal protection under the Fourteenth Amendment. Members of Congress have an opportunity to rectify this practice, which is not utilized in any other democracy, and to restore voting rights to those who have repaid their debt to society as defined by law and common practice.

Reform Proposal #3:
Take Theodore Roosevelt's Advice from 1907

Political campaigns have been expensive entities throughout history, and President Theodore Roosevelt articulated this reality in his State of the Union address on December 3, 1907, when he argued that campaign contributions had to be regulated by Congress in order to protect the greater common good. In this famous speech he endorsed the concept of publicly financed federal campaigns:

> Under our form of government voting is not merely a right but a duty, and, moreover, a fundamental and necessary duty if a man is to be a good citizen. It is well to provide that corporations shall not contribute to Presidential or National campaigns, and furthermore to provide for the publication of both contributions and expenditures. There is, however, always danger in laws of this kind, which from their very nature are difficult of enforcement; that danger being lest they be obeyed only by the honest, and disobeyed by the unscrupulous, so as to act only as a penalty upon honest men. Moreover, no such law would hamper an unscrupulous man

of unlimited means from buying his own way into office. There is a very radical measure which would, I believe, work a substantial improvement in our system of conducting a campaign, although I am well aware that it will take some time for people so to familiarize themselves with such a proposal as to be willing to consider its adoption. The need for collecting large campaign funds would vanish if Congress provided an appropriation for the proper and legitimate expenses of each of the great national parties, an appropriation ample enough to meet the necessity for thorough organization and machinery, which requires a large expenditure of money. Then the stipulation should be made that no party receiving campaign funds from the Treasury should accept more than a fixed amount from any individual subscriber or donor; and the necessary publicity for receipts and expenditures could without difficulty be provided.[22]

Public financing is a system under which federal candidates use funds from the U.S. Treasury to fund their campaigns. Since 1971 funds have been available to presidential candidates only, but to use them they must agree to conform to a complicated set of guidelines. Such funds have never been available to members of Congress.[23]

It took members of Congress sixty-four years to heed Theodore Roosevelt's advice, but they did so only in the presidential electoral arena. It is time to apply his idea to congressional campaigns as well. Members of Congress simply spend too much time fund-raising and not enough time governing and making public policy. Citizens perceive that the 535 voting members of Congress spend hours each day asking for contributions from the very people they are supposed to be regulating. This is part of the reason why the approval rating of Congress has been so low for the past few years. Citizens envision recalcitrant members of Congress doing nothing about the status quo except to enhance their fund-raising capabilities once they finally succeed in getting the job. Fortunately, there are some tangible ideas to rectify this malady. Representative John Yarmuth (D-Ky.) introduced the Fair Elections Now Act at the beginning of 2013. This proposal combines aspects of state measures enacted in Arizona, Connecticut, and Maine as well as the small-donor matching fund program in New York City. If adopted, the program would provide grants of public funds to House candidates. The basic premise is that participating candidates would be permitted to raise small contributions of one hundred dollars or less, and these donations would be matched with additional public funds at a five-to-one ratio.[24] Such a system would allow candidates who use it to compete more vigorously against well-financed incumbents in particular. A diverse populace would witness a grassroots political renaissance, and federal legislators would be much better positioned to pass policies that would promote the general welfare of grateful citizens all across the country.

Reform Proposal #4: Reinvigorate Political Parties and Reform Primaries in the United States

During World War II Professor E. E. Schattschneider offered a conclusion about U.S. political parties:

> The rise of political parties is indubitably one of the principal distinguishing marks of modern government. The parties, in fact, have played a major role as makers of governments, more especially they have been the makers of democratic government. It should be stated flatly at the outset that this volume is devoted to the thesis that the political parties created democracy and that modern democracy is unthinkable save in terms of the parties. As a matter of fact, the condition of the parties is the best possible evidence of the nature of any regime. The most important distinction in modern political philosophy, the distinction between de-

mocracy and dictatorship, can be made best in terms of party politics. The parties are not therefore merely appendages of modern government; they are in the center of it and play a determinative and creative role in it.[25]

Although many Americans view political parties with disdain, Schattschneider's prophecy has profound implications in the real world of politics today. Strong (not corrupt) parties perform a vital role in a democracy. Party leaders present a public policy and philosophical platform and a slate of candidates to the voters. The voters, clear about the parties and their stances on the issues, can subsequently endorse or reject the policies and candidates put forth by party leaders.[26]

This advocacy for stronger, and therefore more accountable, political parties was reiterated in 1950 by members of a committee on political parties of the American Political Science Association. The primary conclusion presented by the authors of the report is still relevant today: "Party responsibility means the responsibility of both parties to the general public, as enforced in elections. Party responsibility to the public, enforced in elections, implies that there be more than one party, for the public can hold a party responsible only if it has a choice. As a means of achieving responsibility, the clarification of party policy also tends to keep public debate on a more realistic level, restraining the inclinations of party spokesmen to make unsubstantiated statements and charges."[27]

The public debate about politics could be far more informed than is presently the case. In the United States, with candidate-centered campaigns, it is very easy to run a campaign full of symbolism with very little substance. Yet such an approach to contesting elections is a disservice to citizens. Those seeking federal office should be equipped to communicate their policy ideas and philosophy of government to the people. One way that Congress could assist in making political parties more responsible to American citizens is to ensure that all states have closed primaries. In a closed primary only voters who are registered with a party can vote in its primary. In open primaries voters of any party affiliation can vote for the slate of candidates of any party.[28] Limiting the primaries to registered voters would enhance the possibility of party discipline in the United States and would provide more clarity to the voters. It is important to understand, however, that citizens play a vital role in the pursuit of more responsible political parties in the United States. American citizens must make politics a higher priority; this can be accomplished by strongly encouraging people to educate themselves about politics and public affairs. Knowledge is a powerful entity in the political world, not unlike any other venue. A more interested, informed, and participatory citizenry will be better positioned to demand more substantive campaigns and be less vulnerable to the politics of manipulation.[29]

In most presidential elections the major party nominees are selected by early March, about eight months before the general election. The primary process is very lengthy, and voters tend to lose interest over time. Members of Congress could intervene and embrace the concept of rotating, regional primaries. I have recommended a modified version of a plan devised in 2008 by the officials at the National Association of Secretaries of State (NASS).[30]

According to the NASS plan the country is divided into four regions: East, South, Midwest, and West. Regional primaries would be held in March, April, May, and June, with the order of regions rotating every four years. A lottery would be conducted initially to determine the order of regions the first time the plan would be implemented. Under the plan two states are omitted (Iowa and New Hampshire) in order to encourage retail politics. In my plan all states would be treated equally. Thus, the groupings are as follows:

East: Connecticut, Delaware, District of Columbia, Maine, Maryland, Massachusetts, New Hampshire, New Jersey, New York, Pennsylvania, Rhode Island, Vermont, and West Virginia (N = 13 states).

Midwest: Illinois, Indiana, Iowa, Kansas, Michigan, Minnesota, Missouri, Nebraska, North Dakota, Ohio, South Dakota, and Wisconsin (N = 12 states).

South: Alabama, Arkansas, Florida, Georgia, Kentucky, Louisiana, Mississippi, North Carolina, Oklahoma, South Carolina, Tennessee, Texas, and Virginia (N = 13 states).

West: Alaska, Arizona, California, Colorado, Hawaii, Idaho, Montana, Nevada, New Mexico, Oregon, Utah, Washington, and Wyoming (N = 13 states).

Having four large primaries during presidential election years would promote more citizen interest and attention to the primary season than is presently the case. A significant objective would be to increase voter turnout in primaries as a result of citizens becoming more engaged in this phase of the presidential electoral contest.

Reform Proposal #5:
Amend the Federal Constitution

The framers of the Constitution debated the issue of presidential selection extensively. The option that they ultimately chose was a reflection of the context of the time period.[31] Direct election was opposed by most of the framers because they questioned the capacity of common citizens to select a suitable chief executive. Congressional selection was also dismissed as a plausible mode of picking a chief executive for fear that this approach would violate the principle of checks and balances. In short, the framers sought to prevent excessive democracy, but that was over 225 years ago. It is time to apply the context of the early twenty-first century to selecting the president.

Citizens across the free world have the right to select their chief executives; Americans lack this fundamental right. Members of Congress need to intervene by passing a constitutional amendment that would allow for direct election and sending it to the states for ratification. The president and vice president would run on the same party ticket, and a threshold of 40 percent would be required for victory. If no candidate garners 40 percent, a runoff election would be held by the two top vote getters thirty days after the general election.[32] Direct election of the president would answer a key question in a democratic manner: first and foremost, is the United States a nation of people or a nation of states? The Electoral College mechanism carves the country into states but not in an equitable manner due to the fact that all states are allocated two U.S. senators, regardless of population. The principle of one person–one vote can only be achieved through direct election by the undifferentiated citizens of the United States.

Summary

To reiterate, members of Congress have embraced democratic reforms to the electoral process in the past and possess the ability to do so now. The tangible effects of such activities would be to continue the nation's pursuit of a more perfect union and to diminish the current cynicism about the people's branch and its ability to get things done. Members of Congress must accept this leadership; doing so will reflect favorably not only on their political legacies but on the current time period in general.

Great contributions to democracy have been crafted in Congress before, and this evolutionary process remains incomplete. The democratic ideal in the United States is worth advancing, and the current members of Congress, in a bipartisan manner, must be proactive and advance the cause of electoral reform now. Democracy requires vigilance, dedication, and a strong work ethic. Because Americans universally embrace the democratic ethos, why not send a positive message of trust to the American people? Tell them that democracy is in their hands, with the full expectation that voting is not only a paramount civil liberty in a free society but a liberty that has serious implications associated with it and one that comes by definition with a great deal of citizen responsibility.

NOTES

1. Gallup Poll, "Congress Approval Ties All-Time Low at 10%," www.gallup.com /poll/156662/Congress-Approval-Ties-Time-Low.aspx (accessed March 20, 2013).

2. Gallup Poll, "Congress Approval Ties All-Time Low at 10%."

3. Gallup Poll, "Congress Approval Ties All-Time Low at 10%"; and Gallup Poll, "Congress and Public Approval: Congressional Job Approval Ratings Trend (1974–present)," www.gallup.com/poll/1600/congress-public.aspx (accessed June 30, 2013).

4. For a more detailed discussion of electoral changes in American history, see Brian L. Fife, *Reforming the Electoral Process in America: Toward More Democracy in the 21st Century* (Santa Barbara, Calif.: ABC-CLIO, 2010), 4–29.

5. Fife, *Reforming the Electoral Process in America*, 13–18.

6. It was stipulated by law that Election Day would be the Tuesday after the first Monday in November for the appointment of presidential electors every four years.

7. Library of Congress, "Statutes at Large, 1789–1875," http://memory.loc.gov /ammem/amlaw/lwsllink.html (accessed March 24, 2013).

8. 2 U.S.C. 7 and 2 U.S.C. 1, respectively.

9. Avalon Project: Documents in Law, History and Diplomacy, Yale Law School, "*The Federalist Papers:* No. 28," http://avalon.law.yale.edu/18th_century/fed28.asp (accessed on April 10, 2013); and Avalon Project, "*The Federalist Papers:* No. 46," http:// avalon.law.yale.edu/18th_century/fed46.asp (accessed on April 10, 2013).

10. *Dunn v. Blumstein,* 405 U.S. 330 (1972).

11. *Dunn v. Blumstein* (1972).

12. Fife, *Reforming the Electoral Process in America*, 36.

13. National Conference of State Legislatures, "Same-Day Voter Registration," www.ncsl.org/legislatures-elections/elections/same-day-registration.aspx (accessed on June 9, 2013); and Project Vote, "Election Day Registration," www.projectvote.org /election-day-reg.html (accessed on April 11, 2013).

14. GovTrack.us, "H.R. 12: Voter Empowerment Act of 2013," www.govtrack.us /congress/bills/113/hr12 (accessed on April 11, 2013).

15. GovTrack.us, "S. 123: Voter Empowerment Act of 2013," www.govtrack.us/con gress/bills/113/s123 (accessed on April 11, 2013).

16. Brennan Center for Justice, "The Case for Voter Registration Modernization," www.brennancenter.org/sites/default/files/publications/Case%20Voter%20Registra tion%20Modernization.pdf (accessed on April 11, 2013).

17. Brennan Center for Justice, "Restoring Voting Rights," www.brennancenter .org/issues/restoring-voting-rights (accessed on April 12, 2013).

18. Brennan Center for Justice, "Criminal Disenfranchisement Laws across the United States," www.brennancenter.org/sites/default/files/legacy/Democracy/RTV %20Map%207.5.12.pdf (accessed on April 12, 2013).

19. Fife, *Reforming the Electoral Process in America*, 39–42.

20. GovTrack.us, "H.R. 2212: Democracy Restoration Act of 2011," www.govtrack .us/congress/bills/112/hr2212 (accessed on April 12, 2013).

21. GovTrack.us, "S. 2017: Democracy Restoration Act of 2011," www.govtrack.us /congress/bills/112/s2017 (accessed on April 13, 2013).

22. American Presidency Project, "Theodore Roosevelt: Seventh Annual Message, December 3, 1907," www.presidency.ucsb.edu/ws/index.php?pid=29548 (accessed on April 13, 2013).

23. Annenberg Public Policy Center, University of Pennsylvania, "What Is Public Financing?" www.factcheck.org/2008/04/what-is-public-financing (accessed April on 13, 2013).

24. Brennan Center for Justice, "Fair Elections Now Act, January 15, 2013," www .brennancenter.org/legislation/fair-elections-now-act (accessed on April 13, 2013); and GovTrack.us, "H.R. 269: Fair Elections Now Act," www.govtrack.us/congress /bills/113/hr269 (accessed on April 13, 2013).

25. E. E. Schattschneider, *Party Government* (New York: Rinehart, 1942), 1.

26. Fife, *Reforming the Electoral Process in America*, 122–26.

27. American Political Science Association, Committee on Political Parties, *Toward a More Responsible Two-Party System* (New York: Rinehart, 1950), 2.

28. FairVote, Center for Voting and Democracy, "Congressional and Presidential

Primaries: Open, Closed, Semi-Closed, and "Top Two,'" www.fairvote.org/congressional-and-presidential-primaries-open-closed-semi-closed-and-top-two (accessed on April 15, 2013).

29. Fife, *Reforming the Electoral Process in America,* 125–26.

30. National Association of Secretaries of State, *The Case for Regional Presidential Primaries in 2012 and Beyond: Report of the NASS Subcommittee on Presidential Primaries,* February 2008, www.nass.org/index.php?option=com_content&do_pdf=1&id=74 (accessed April 15, 2013).

31. Fife, *Reforming the Electoral Process in America,* 71–85.

32. Fife, *Reforming the Electoral Process in America,* 133–35.

Voices of Former Members of Congress

Former Senator Tom Daschle (D-S.Dak.): You look at 1917 to 1967, if I recall, we had 52 cloture votes in a little over fifty years. I believe the number was 52. We had 112 cloture votes in the 111th Congress, and so we had twice as many in one Congress as we did in fifty years.

I think there are two things that really could at least be considered. One is that we now dual and triple and quadruple [legislative] track. When there's a filibuster, we set the bill aside, and we take up another bill. We have diminished the pain involved with a filibuster simply by saying we're not going to use time on the floor to make that happen, and I think that really is a factor that has minimized the impact of a filibuster, and that's why there are so many.

We thought it was a reform. It's really not, but dual and triple tracking—that is, setting the bill aside and just taking up something else—is one thing that we ought to reconsider.

The second thing is holding the floor. If people really had to hold the floor and retain the recognition of the floor during that time they're filibustering, it could really also alter the dynamic that occurs. You are not required to keep the floor any longer, and those two factors have really changed the dynamics of filibusters, dual tracking and not being required to hold the floor any longer.

Former Senator Trent Lott (R-Miss.): You should always consider ways that you can do a better job. Reform of the institution of the rules is something that you shouldn't just reject out of hand, but as you might expect, I say be careful what you wish for because you might get it.

You know, I do believe that the Senate is a unique institution, and you do look for supermajorities. It can happen. You know, Tom [Daschle] and I used to try to do some reforms. We found you had to do it gingerly. We had a problem with holds. This is one of the things that makes senators nervous, and that is some freshman senator shows up now, and he figures it out real quick, or she does: "Hey, I can stop this whole damn institution. I can impose a hold, and by the way, I'll go back to my office and hide where they can't find me." It used to be they didn't even have to acknowledge that they were doing it.

Tom and I on two occasions tried to reform the hold, to at least make your senator do it himself or herself and acknowledge that they were doing it, a few things like that. . . . I always had a problem, frankly, with a filibuster on the motion to proceed. What you were saying is, "I don't want to even debate the issue." I would be inclined ordinarily to let that go, and if you're going to filibuster a bill, filibuster the bill itself.

So, you can always look for some reforms, but I do think that there is a uniqueness [to the Senate]. When you get the Senate to come up with a super vote—sixty-one or sixty or seventy—more than likely you pulled the country together with you. I think that's one of the problems we've had with Obamacare. It passed by such a close margin, it was so partisan, and the nation was divided fifty-fifty, without getting into the substance. I think that's one of the problems that we've had. We never really got enough input.

I don't say the Republicans weren't to blame for some of that because they wouldn't engage to a degree. Those who did try to engage, like [former senator] Olympia Snowe [R-Maine], wound up getting hammered.

So, I just say, on reform, you should always think about what you can do, but just like Democrats, I would warn now if you change the filibuster rule and if the Republicans someday do come back in the majority, then it's going to work against you.

I also feel like that we should look at ways to improve the confirmation process. It's ridiculous. [Senator Charles] Schumer [D-N.Y.] and Senator Lamar Alexander [R-Tenn.] came up with a plan to take three hundred–and–something nominations to commissions and bureaus out of the confirmation process, but I think we should look at that a little bit more.

You know, there are a lot of Obama administration nominees up there right now I'd vote against, but I would make sure that they had the vote. And I really think that the president is entitled to his cabinet. Even if you struggle with voting for them. It's just like on Supreme Court nominees. I voted for Justice [Ruth Bader] Ginsburg. I knew philosophically I wouldn't agree with her, but she met the basic criteria. She was qualified. She had a good demeanor. So, I couldn't bring myself to vote against her, but I got hammered because I voted for her.

5

Can't We All Just Get Along?
Civility and Bipartisanship in Congress
Susan Herbst

Congressional discourse tends to mirror the larger social and economic dynamics of any period, and our current era is no exception. Members of both houses do in fact represent the electorate that sent them to Washington as well as the more general contours of American culture. It would be inaccurate to say that the behavior of our representatives, in any period, dictates or even directs the nature of public discourse or the level of civility we see. As many have noted, Congress is a reflection of who we are as a nation, not a body of distinguished strangers who have arrived from a higher and wiser strata to serve as role models. We might like to signal the latter case to schoolchildren, but the reality is that members are embedded in the nature of the times in the same ways that we all are. To face this reality head on enables the sort of analyses we need if we are to shape a legislature we can admire—or at least live with comfortably—into the future.

The original title of this chapter—"Restoring Civility and Bipartisanship to Congress"—is not one that I would have chosen because it implies that Congress was once highly civil and that we have been on a downward decline. Such a reading of congressional or American history could not be further from the truth because incivility has been a *constant* both in our elected bodies and in broader political life. It may be fashionable to say that this is the worse incivility we have ever seen, but we know the claim to be false.

The eighteenth, nineteenth, and early twentieth centuries were far more brutal with regard to congressional behavior. In fact, I chose a lithograph of the famous caning of Senator Charles Sumner of Massachusetts by Congressman Preston Brooks of South Carolina for my book on civility and incivility. As many of you know, that 1856 incident was an excellent example of the animosity over slavery that characterized the 1850s, a real low point—without question the rock bottom—of the United States as a democracy. The nastiness of Congress was actually downplayed in the 2012 motion picture *Lincoln*. In the years before the Civil War, fistfights, brawls, and ugly language were commonplace in Washington, and while trying to cane someone to death was a bit over the top, it was not exactly unexpected. Senator Sumner lived through his severe injuries, barely, and Congressman Brooks of South Carolina became a legendary southern hero. I often refer to the caning and incidents like it to try to fight against the "golden age" argument: that members of Congress, and the country as a whole, were once quite gentlemanly and civil and that we are now in a horrible period as a result of a linear decline in manners and respect.

I am not arguing that this is a wonderful or even good era; it certainly is not. But there have been lengthy periods of both civility and incivility in American history. We have moved from one to the other and back again, if one takes the long view of history. Maybe that does not give much comfort in the very unhappy status quo of the present day. But it should underscore the fact that incivility has been a chronic phenomenon in American history, dormant or absent in some eras but then omnipresent in others. In fact, Rod Hart, my good colleague at the University of Texas, has argued that incivility is quite *functional* for us, even attractive to us, which is why it never quite goes away. More on that later, but suffice it to say we have always witnessed bad behavior and worrisome conflict—what I call "rude democracy."[1]

I am not a scholar of Congress or congressional history and of course will never understand the day-to-day work and pressure one feels as a member of Congress. In fact, I read the political science literature on Congress with a degree of skepticism because understanding the body is only truly accomplished by those who have had the courage and ability to serve. Understanding Congress likely calls for more contributions from sociology and anthropology than currently exist because Congress is made of the very same fabric as American culture itself. And that is what makes it so interesting to those of us who study civility and incivility from a broad, macro-historical perspective.

I will stick more closely to the issue of civility than bipartisanship because I know more about it. And I believe the roots of bipartisanship, or lack thereof, are well studied in the academy and by journalists. We all understand, for example, that state legislatures have been redistricting in ways that lead to more extremist candidates being elected to Congress. And there are other cultural factors that have made bipartisanship difficult, from the nature of members' lifestyles (spending more time in the district/state and less time in Washington; not moving families to the capital) to the personalities and ideologies of the leadership. I imagine that bipartisanship is at base very much like civility: it is not a cyclical phenomenon but rises and falls, keyed to the economy, terrorism threats, war, and less dramatic but important events and waves affecting our culture.

Here I want to broaden the discussion of civility and incivility in Congress, so that we can depart from the golden age and linear decline arguments, which are simply not true. I will break the remainder of this chapter into three sections, addressing incivility as a weapon in American life, the role of the media in the dynamics of incivility, and last, our fear and confusion about the nature of argument. Finally, I will offer some solutions, primarily through the lens of educators, who are very conscious of the sorts of citizens we create, in higher education and in our K–12 schools.

Incivility as a Strategic Rhetorical Tool

As I note in *Rude Democracy*, reviewing the extensive scholarly literature on the history of manners and civility, incivility has always been present in American culture and politics. Our Founding Fathers were not angels at all but were ambitious politicians, and they fought with each other, often quite viciously. They used nasty names and the worst sorts of personal accusations they could get away with. A fascinating example is Thomas Jefferson's lengthy battle with provincial authorities and clergy to build the University of Virginia in which he used language and tactics we university people would be appalled at today.[2]

And the incivility kept coming throughout our history, certainly in the extraordinarily dark decade before the Civil War but then well into the twentieth century. Veteran journalist and former White House press secretary Bill Moyers and his coauthor Michael Winship noted in 2012 that former Florida representative Allen West sounded much like Senator Joseph McCarthy in calling out current members of Congress as being communists.[3] This is a bizarre apples-to-apples resonance across decades, but the point is that incivility was practiced by McCarthy then and still gets practiced today.

I have argued that political civility and incivility are best looked at as weapons in one's rhetorical arsenal, not as *states* of a society. It would be difficult to posit, and impossible to prove empirically, that we are in either a civil period or an uncivil period in any case. We cannot easily imagine a societal civility "scale" on which to rate different decades or people, given that contexts change so mightily. Actions or words that might be clearly uncivil in one period might not look or feel so bad to people in another. Or to make it even more difficult, ever-expanding media make it increasingly possible to hear more and see more from our fellow citizens, so the sheer size of the public opinion "universe" keeps expanding decade by decade. The world felt much more civil back when we didn't hear as many opinions as we do today.

Civility and incivility are rhetorical mechanisms we use when we argue, for good or not-so-good purposes. What if we looked at our congressional leaders as using tools of both civility and incivility to get what they want? I believe that most leaders are complex in motive and that their methods are far more fluid than we generally recognize. One very fine example is the candidacy for U.S. vice president of Sarah Palin, whom I wrote about in my book. You may admire her or disdain her, but a close look at her campaign reveals tremendous civility and warmth as well as vicious red meat–flinging incivility. So, was she civil, or was she uncivil? This depended on the venue and audience. She was a politician trying to win and score her points, and she used incivility as she thought she needed to do so.

This is a controversial way to look at things, I realize. It does excuse some unattractive and often unproductive public behavior. But it also has the effect of making us far less upset and emotional when we hear uncivil dialogue because we see it as a strategic weapon or asset, not the essence of someone's character or the tenor of the times. Again, hard to swallow, but this way of viewing incivility takes significant pain out of the concept and intellectualizes it in a way that lets us talk with fewer hurt feelings. In our daily lives—dealing with our teenagers, for example—we may hear some rotten things that we cannot imagine we'll ever forget. But we know they are lovely, too, and so we treat them as whole, if flawed, people who use a variety of rhetorical and behavioral tactics to get what they want. Perhaps we should think of politicians in the same way, instead of unproductively bemoaning this or that nasty comment or set of accusations. Who cares that John Boehner said the "*F* word" in the White House during the fiscal cliff trauma of early January 2013? Was that really so awful, given the level of frustration on all sides?

Media Responsibility?

My second point is that we might want to blame Congress less and put a bit more responsibility on our media professionals. After all, members of Congress are in the heat of battle. They are ideological, aggravated, tired, angry, and trying to get done what they believe is the right thing. Of course, many are cynical, but they always have been, cynicism being another constant in American political life since our founding, hardly a new phenomenon.

I do not believe that there is any question that incivility serves the media—all outlets but cable news in particular—very well. Incivility in Congress, or anywhere else, makes for exciting coverage for news broadcasts, talk shows, and comedy programs. Journalists and their editors have decided, consciously at times, unconsciously at others, that audiences will fall asleep without conflict, and the more personal and bitter the better.

Researchers studying incivility in media programming, labeling it "outrage discourse" (name-calling, mockery, deliberate misrepresentation, etc.), have found it in the large majority of talk radio programs, cable news broadcasts, as well as political blogs. While it is difficult to make a longitudinal argument about changing media, given the conflation of technology and content (there was no cable news a few decades ago, and the Internet did not exist), it is instructive that outrage characterizes so much framing of content.[4] Not all of it is problematic, and we have little evidence of how an audience processes the information. But the omnipresence of outrage and incivility is instructive and certainly overwhelms the amount of incivility one finds in the typical congressional day.

We should make a distinction here between the conventional journalism of the network news and the content of cable news, different in some ways and not in others. They are both excited by the drama and melodrama of incivility, as it makes for a more interesting broadcast. But the network news, by nature of its conventions, tends to be less hysterical even if the essential coverage is the same. In any case we do need to focus on cable news as well as the Internet because the cohort of Americans dependent on the nightly news is aging out of the population, replaced by younger people who rely on cable news and the Internet.[5]

It is impossible to argue with any confidence for a unidirectional, causal link: that the media cause either public incivility or congressional incivility. But their role is obviously vital in producing this result and leads one to valuable theoretical questions—in particular: *Would Congress seem so uncivil if journalists and pundits didn't constantly underscore incivility and seek it out?* This is doubtful. I rarely see video clips of an accommodating or civil speech on the House or Senate floor, although they are what dominate the hours of talk in the chambers and committee meetings daily. No one person or influential media outlet ever decided to accelerate the focus on uncivil speech in Congress; it is simply a natural result of increased competition for a highly segmented audience. Economics dictate the nature of media content, and if the excitement of incivility draws in the viewers, one cannot blame a worried editor or network manager for using it to their advantage.

Fear of Argument

The last major point I want to make before briefly offering some new ideas is one that does not always sit well with my colleagues: perhaps incivility is overblown as a problem in American culture, and the central issue is how thin-skinned we have become in our daily social and political lives.

We do, after all, live in a culture in which self-esteem and good feeling are predominant notions that dictate our policies and actions. As someone who has spent a lifetime in higher education, as a professor and a leader, I can tell you that college students and their parents have changed tremendously over the decades. It is of utmost import that students are treated with kid gloves, that no one offends anyone, and that no one is made to feel inadequate. On the whole this is very nice, but it has crushed argumentation as a driving force in the academy, particularly in the classroom.

Professors argue hard with each other; we always have, and we probably always will. But the feeling in a classroom now is quite guarded. When I have taught in recent years, I have been very cautious to always be bipartisan, to give students a comfort level in discussion, and not to say anything too outrageous or challenging for fear that I will be reported to a dean. Also, there is the added fear of being recorded, your remarks taken out of context, and making an appearance on YouTube somehow. Professors can't risk this exposure anymore, especially when they are teaching politically charged subjects, and so they've lowered their standard for argumentation in class.

As a result, we teach argument poorly or not at all. I found, in conducting a two-year study of thousands of college students, that they want to avoid argument and conflict at all costs. Here are quotes from two different students, both making the point—that argument is uncomfortable and even scary. The first wrote: "The number of times I've seen students almost become violent with another student over politics is a big factor in why I think many students either aren't respectful or just don't care. From personal experience, I've been verbally attacked quite a few times for my political stance, despite being sure to [choose] my words carefully so as to not cause offense."[6] Another wrote: "Whenever there are several diverse groups of people in a certain place, respect generally decreases. While there are many people that are respectful of others and their views, there are also many that criticize due to having a different opinion than their own. At my institution, there are people from many different cultures, races and economic standings . . . [Politics] is a very touchy subject for many, and a conversation between people of different political beliefs would more than likely turn into a very heated and disrespectful debate."[7]

This fear of argument and discomfort is hardly confined to university students, as anyone who has worked in an office day to day understands. It is well known by social scientists that people selectively expose themselves to others who they already know agree with them. When you are certain that a discussion of, say, health care will set off a debate with a colleague that might get uncomfortable, it is typically avoided. As many people have pointed out to me, extended family gatherings are often the very worst moments to approach controversial issues. Who wants to ruin Thanksgiving dinner when you know that your sister-in-law is fiercely on the other end of the ideological continuum from you? Better just to avoid politics altogether, figure out a way to have a more banal discussion, or selectively talk with your relatives!

A conundrum, then, is that we—college students and those who are much older—avoid argument in daily life but then turn happily to cable television to see generally juvenile and poor argumentation. What is missing are models for passionate argument that may now and then become uncivil but are still largely productive and gratifying. Some incivility is tolerable, and indeed appropriate, if the bulk of discourse is intelligent and evidence based. Alas, my students, and all citizens, find themselves shuttling back and forth between interpersonal situations in which they fear argument and viewing media and blogs in which idiotic and uncivil argument dominates the content.

Some Ways Forward for Citizens and for Congress

In my book on civility I propose the extensive teaching of argument and cite a variety of wonderful tools on the Internet that so many innovative teachers have shared. While we often push the teaching of citizenship onto K–12 educators, escaping that responsibility in higher education, it is the case that early experience with argumentation is extraordinarily valuable in developing democratic hearts and minds. Instead of bland lessons in public speaking or how to use PowerPoint, we should teach young people how to develop their passions and then argue with force and evidence. The earlier we can teach students how to argue with passion and respect, the more practiced they will be with these tools as they advance to adulthood.

The other side of teaching argumentation is teaching students how to listen. There are some exemplary projects in the public sphere, such as NPR's *StoryCorps*, but on the whole listening is largely underplayed as a skill vitally needed in developing democratic citizens. Political programming on cable television tends to suppress listening, as various ideologues make their arguments. The result is typically both poor argumentation (scattered, passionate, but without linearity or evidence) and poor or nonexistent listening. A conversation cannot advance, on policy or any other matter, without both argumentation and keen listening, or ideas will lay undeveloped, of course. And neither party learns much.

A population taught those two things—arguing and listening—will over time produce a better electorate and therefore a better Congress. But what might be done sooner?

The Annenberg Public Policy Center has tracked congressional rules already in place, and some forms of unproductive discourse have disappeared, while other, less productive behaviors live on.[8] But perhaps Congress itself can do a better job by developing it own public relations approach, figuring out a compelling and efficient way to broadcast the very civil debate that occurs there each day. Few citizens have the time or patience for C-SPAN, but I imagine that there are ways to underscore, through interesting and sustained video montage, the collegiality and civility that characterizes much of legislative life. If congressional leaders leave the portrayal of Congress entirely up to *The Daily Show* or cable news, they are at the mercy of those characterizations.

I leave these notions to scholars of Congress and legislators themselves. But the sorts of pedagogical changes I recommend, ones that will create better citizens capable of more sophisticated argumentation and listening, would have a profound effect in my view. It is worth the time and energy: changing the fundamental "culture of argument" in our schools and colleges will eventually shape a larger discourse in our institutions—the media, Congress, workplaces, and so many others.

NOTES

1. Roderick Hart, UConn Metanoia Program on Civility, University of Connecticut, September 5, 2012; Susan Herbst, *Rude Democracy: Civility and Incivility in American Politics* (Philadelphia: Temple University Press, 2012).

2. Garry Wills, *Mr. Jefferson's University* (Washington, D.C.: National Geographic, 2002).

3. Bill Moyers and Michael Winship, "The Ghost of Joe McCarthy Slithers Again," *Moyers and Company,* "On Democracy," April 26, 2012, http://billmoyers.com /2012/04/26/the-ghost-of-joe-mccarthy-slithers-again/ (accessed on September 19, 2013).

4. Sarah Sobieraj and Jeffrey M. Berry, "From Incivility to Outrage: Political Discourse in Blogs, Talk Radio, and Cable News," *Political Communication* 28, no. 1 (2011): 19–41.

5. Andrew Beaujon, "Pew: Half of Americans Get News Digitally, Topping Newspapers, Radio," Poynter.org, www.poynter.org/latest-news/mediawire/189819/pew -tv-viewing-habit-grays-as-digital-news-consumption-tops-print-radio/ (accessed on September 19, 2013).

6. Herbst, *Rude Democracy,* 114–15.

7. Herbst, *Rude Democracy,* 115.

8. Annenberg Public Policy Center, "Civility in the House of Representatives: The 106th Congress," www.annenbergpublicpolicycenter.org/Downloads/Civility/Old%20 reports/2001_civility106th.pdf (accessed on September 19, 2013).

Voices of Former Members of Congress

Former Senator Byron Dorgan (D-N.Dak.): The House was created and structured to represent the passions of the moment and the politics of the day. So that's not unusual that the House would be more partisan than the Senate, generally speaking, but I think there's very little change or very little difference these days [between the House and Senate], except in the two-year versus the six-year term, with talk radio, cable television, and particularly social media now. It is real-time politics for everybody. It doesn't matter what that last vote was. That last vote on all the social media devices and the communication capabilities put senators not in a six-year cocoon where it's not going to matter so much, not going to notice so much. It's the same in the House and the Senate in terms of the introspection of how this person is behaving, are they . . . to be punished for compromising or rewarded for obstruction?

This communication cycle that we're in has had a profound impact, I think, on the way both the House and the Senate behave.

Former Senator Trent Lott (R-Miss.): Another thing that Tom [Daschle] and I used to do, we talked. Occasionally, we would help each other, run interference with each other, but also every now and then I'd do something I shouldn't have done, like fill up the tree where there could be no amendments offered. First time I did that, I thought Tom was going to blow a gasket.

We actually apologized to each other occasionally. We actually confessed our sins to each other, which tends to bond you, and I think maybe we had a unique relationship, but, boy, it sure helps when you have leaders who do really kind of like each other and feel like we got to find a way to get things done.

Former Senator Tom Daschle (D-S.Dak.): It's so true. I mean, Trent and I have become very, very close friends, and I treasure the friendship.

Another thing we haven't really talked about—and I may be the only one who thinks this—but I do think the primary process today in both parties is also influencing the next generation of people who are getting elected. We've seen indications of that recently.

The primary becomes the more important of the two elections. The primaries back in the '60s and '70s were considered a reform. It gave the people more of an opportunity to have a voice. But because of low voter turnout in primaries, it's not hard to capture the majority in a primary election. And so, groups on the Far Left and the Far Right are doing that with greater frequency and success, and that elects a different person when the primary becomes the more important of the two elections. We have got to figure out ways to ensure that the general election is still the most important of the two elections.

6

Is Persuasion a Lost Art?
How Members of Congress Can Stop Shouting and Start Persuading
Mark Kennedy

No one can become a member of Congress without persuading a sizable portion of a district's population (usually beginning with a spouse) that he or she should be their representative in Washington, D.C. While this effort has increasingly included a lot of shouting, it is nevertheless an intense competition for who can be the most persuasive in advancing their cause. Why, then, does it appear that the art of persuasion escapes elected officials once they enter the chambers of the U.S. Capitol? It appears that contention and gridlock rule the day.

Many pine for the days when President Ronald Reagan and House Speaker Tip O'Neill would fight by day yet share a few drinks and laughs at night. Some suggest that it is simply that members of Congress don't socialize enough together.

My own view is that the hurdles to reaching national consensus have gotten immensely higher since the days of Reagan and O'Neill's congeniality. It is not the case that today's members are less skilled at persuasion than those of Reagan's years. It is because lawmakers face more significant obstacles to collaboration, and their skills have not improved enough.

In order to address this malady, we must first examine the hurdles that make it more difficult for congressmen and women to persuade each other. Then I will propose new approaches to reactivate the effectiveness of persuasion in advancing legislative aims.

Traditional Hurdles

Before we examine the hurdles that have gone up since Reagan's day, here are two classic hurdles that are foundational to the consensus-building challenge for national issues: the basic structures of public opinion and campaigning.

1. The "Most People Agree with Me" Hurdle

Most people's average day is composed of interactions with family, friends, and coworkers whose views they either share or don't discuss in order to maintain harmony. As a result, they are left with the impression that most people agree with them. That bias leads them to believe that the source of gridlock in Washington is that members of Congress are an unusually contentious lot, unlike the population from which they emerge.

Even if it is true that most people with whom one person interacts agree, the "most people" in Boston have a radically different view from the "most people" in Houston. And because few of the people in Boston and Houston have had a chance to mingle in both worlds, most people in fact have little sense of just how different their views really are from much of the rest of the nation.

Nowhere is this "most people" difference more crystal clear than in Congress. In a democracy representatives reflect their constituencies. As such, the representatives of suburban Boston and Houston reflect their respective populations and agree on almost nothing. Public opinion polling regularly shows voters support their own member of Congress more than Congress generally, reflecting a lack of perception and appreciation for the rich variety of viewpoints held by the American electorate.

In the end it is the widely divergent views among Americans that is the source of the conflict exhibited in Washington, D.C. This is a fundamental that is not likely to change. As Rutgers professor Ross Baker said at the 2013 John Breaux Symposium, "Nothing short of replacing the electorate would solve the problem."

2. Campaigning Hurdle

Another factor that contributes to the difficulty of reaching congressional consensus is derived from the fact that the formative experience of any member of Congress is winning an election. Depending on the district or state, the pivotal contest will be either the primary or the general election. At a minimum one of these venues is usually highly competitive during a member's first race. A standard formula for winning these contests is first to define who you are and then to persuade targeted segments of voters that, among the alternatives, you are most on their side and most capable of representing their worldview.

While candidates' general campaign themes may purport that they will reach across the aisle and get things done, the messages they transmit to their key constituencies will center on the fact that they will hold fast to shared values or goals. It becomes quite clear to successful candidates that decisive portions of their electorate will abandon them if they do not stay true to their commitments on issues such as abortion, guns, marriage, taxes, entitlements, and many more. Congressional representatives soon learn that persuading these voting blocs to support their reelection does not require advanced oratorical skills; simply refusing to bend on the issue at hand will be enough. As a result, members of Congress do not really require advanced persuasion skills to regularly win reelection; their elementary approach to persuading voting blocs raises significant hurdles to their ability to persuade each other to come to the middle on an issue.

Higher Hurdles

Those two traditional hurdles members of Congress face aren't new and have not changed much in recent years. The reason the virility of gridlock has escalated is because other hurdles have arisen or become more pronounced in recent decades, making the challenge of reaching consensus much more difficult. An understanding of the higher hurdles those seeking action face will also shine light on the new skills they require. While new difficulties are legion, these are the six highest new hurdles for elected officials.

1. From Lopsided Democratic Majority to Neck and Neck

As University of Maryland professor Frances Lee noted during the Breaux Symposium, discussion of structural changes to Congress to encourage bipartisan cooperation, when the Democrats' majority was so large that there was no prospect for a change of control, the disincentive for Republicans to collaborate with Democrats was smaller. Ever since the historic Republican takeover of the U.S. House of Representatives after a forty-year drought in 1994, control of the levers of power always seemed within reach in the next election for the minority party. With both parties being neck and neck and control of Congress hanging in the balance when considering every issue, there is now little incentive to compromise.

Solution: Because unilateral surrender is not a trait admired in America, it is unlikely there is any solution for this obstacle to cooperation until one side gains a sizable and sustainable electoral edge over the other.

2. The Self-Selected Media Hurdle

Gone are the days when everyone got his or her news from one of three news networks, all with a similar slant on the events of the day.

Actually, when I grew up in northern Minnesota, we only got one channel: NBC. In college I would hear references to shows like *Leave It to Beaver* that I had never seen. Today's media is much more fragmented, offering thousands of alternative choices to inform one's worldview.

People don't order vanilla if they prefer chocolate. A similar pattern of choosing news sources that reinforce personal preferences has led to an increasingly polarized electorate, largely unaware of the fundamental chasms that divide citizens. This fragmentation of media allows individuals to stay in their cocoons. Most voters would have difficulty articulating points of view contrary to their own. Figuring out why anyone would ever want to embrace an opposing viewpoint would be a Herculean mental feat for many. A mushrooming of news sources has amplified this hurdle to consensus building.

This more pronounced segmentation of society has been exploited by political campaigns through increasingly sophisticated microtargeting. The advent of Big Data has allowed campaigns to appeal to individual voters by pulling heartstrings they deduce from the extensive information that is knowable about each of us online.

Solution: Is there much likelihood that voter perceptions of the public at large will become more complete over time? Not likely. Can you take a forced busing approach to broaden individuals' media horizons? Of course not! The most productive effort would be to educate elected officials in the art of appealing to a more complete spectrum of the electorate in order to advance their goals. This will make them better politicians. When we address elevated persuasive skills, we will address the path to "Seeing 360° and Speaking 360°."

3. The Gerrymandering Hurdle

There is no doubt that one area in which members of Congress have become more skilled is in managing the redistricting process to secure their own reelection. As a result, the number of swing districts has dwindled from 103 in 1992 to only 35 in 2012.[1] Today the vast majority of House members are more worried about a primary challenge than a general election. They have little incentive to be seen fraternizing with the other side. Doing so may create an opening for a primary opponent to topple them in a safe district.

Solution: Unfortunately, gerrymandering complaint season peaks just after redistricting is complete. In order to reduce this hurdle to congressional consensus, it is imperative to identify the approaches that lead to the most balanced districts and form effective coalitions to advocate for their implementation. This effort should start well in advance of the next round of district revisions following the 2020 census.

4. Misguided Campaign Finance Reform Hurdle

Many feel that money is the root of the problem in politics. This view fails, however, to consider all the distortions that have been enacted as a result of attempts to limit money in politics. Campaign finance restrictions have not limited the money in politics; they have, contrary to proponents' wishes, pushed it into less transparent entities. By limiting the amount an individual or political action committee (PAC) can give to a candidate, money first flowed to the parties. Then new restrictions limited contributions to the parties, which sparked the rise of Super PACs. History would suggest that any limits on Super PACs will only spark fresh innovation that will push the nexus of money even further from the moderating element of a candidate disclosing that they "approve this message."

Many demonize political parties as the source of division. This line of thought maintains that if individual representatives were simply allowed to go their own way, different mixtures of members would coalesce around solutions to our pressing problems. It seems to me that it is equally likely that the legislative process would descend into chaos if no parties existed. The critics overlook the fact that parties can be an effective unifying force that facilitates action. As Super PACs have replaced the role of parties, their multiplicity and variety have pulled candidates in increasingly divergent directions, making it harder for them to agree with each other once in office. The resulting breakdown in party control has made Congress more dysfunctional, causing former congressman Norm Dicks (D-Wash.) to complain that the majority in the U.S. House of Representatives is having trouble fulfilling its "duty to deliver 218 votes."[2]

Solution: Rather than trying to limit contributions and dictate how money can be spent, a more effective solution would be to let individual candidates' money spigots flow as freely as possible but require them to show immediately where their wells are located. Let each candidate consider whether he or she can still get elected if everyone knows this candidate took a million dollars from any one individual, industry, or union. Doing so will have the impact of having more of the money being funneled through activities for which the candidate themselves can be held directly accountable. Because candidates would feel as if they were more in control of their own destinies, rather than just being puppets of Super PACs, the change would also hopefully attract higher-quality candidates with the skills and temperament to seek solutions.

5. The Rise of Activism

Although not a child of the rebellious 1960s, I grew up in its aftermath. That period sparked a focus on ensuring that all voices were heard in the public debate. There should be little doubt that more voices are included today than in earlier decades when considering nearly any issue on the national stage. This is a positive and essential development, but it does make it harder to reach consensus. It is harder to get twenty people to agree on dinner plans than three. The same applies to achieving legislative agreement.

The challenges for consensus building with the addition of more voices has been compounded by fact that some of these new voices are more interested in hearing themselves speak than in having a discussion. My friend Nate Garvis, an avowed independent, former head of external relations for a major U.S. retailer and now the head of Naked Civics (whose purpose is "to strip away the politics to build a better world"), calls these elements the "outrage industry that gets paid by the fight and can't take yes for an answer."[3] Indeed, some activist organizations' existence depends upon sufficient outrage over specific problems generating an ongoing stream of contributions to cover their costs.

Yet the phrase *outrage industry* doesn't give a complete picture of the activist community, which includes many very different organizations with wide-ranging focuses and approaches. Some of these activist groups can be forces for good and should be empowered to serve as counterweights to the rage-fomenting organizations. Leaving aside any judgment about whether any one organization is a worthy enterprise or not, there is no doubt they represent more significant challenges to reaching agreement today than during Reagan's presidency.

Solution: Include those activist organizations willing to collaborate in your coalitions and find ways to turn down the volume on groups that just want to make noise.

6. Heavier Political Lift Hurdle

The issues Congress faces today are far more challenging politically than those faced by past congresses. In the past the legislature could end an impasse by deferring tough choices and just spending a little more to make Democrats happy and cutting a few more taxes to make Republicans happy. The nation's current fiscal situation prevents this strategy today and forces lawmakers to overcome political challenges that in the past they would have avoided.

Additionally, when combined with a divided nation, the rules of the institution can be a hurdle to consensus. The requirement in the Senate to obtain a sixty-vote supermajority to proceed with legislation has long slowed action in the upper chamber. While it is within the power of the body to change this requirement, it persists because it protects the majority from having to take highly controversial votes, gives the minority leverage, and adheres to Thomas Jefferson's maxim that "Great innovations should not be forced on a slender majority."

In the House, where a simple majority is enough to pass legislation, the rules empower leadership. Historically, this has led to more partisan results, though House members tend to develop relationships with the opposition party members they work with in legislative committees. As a result, advancing legislation through committee procedures often generates a less partisan bill. But as the legislative process in the House has become more centralized in recent congresses, the role of committees has diminished, exacerbating the partisan nature of the institution.

Congress has also eliminated the use of earmarks, depriving party leaders in the House and Senate of a useful tool to gain votes. Those targeted spending measures made it easier to grease the congressional gears to get bills passed. Leaving aside the question of whether halting earmarks was good policy, their absence makes it harder to find ways to get hesitant lawmakers off the fence.

It is useful to study the Wilson-Lowi Matrix to better understand why today's issues are more difficult to face. The matrix "categorized the nature of political competition on an issue as a function of the concentration or dispersion of the benefits and costs from an alternative . . . relative to the status quo . . . The benefits or harm are said to be concentrated if the per capita effects are high" and low if widely dispersed.[4] The matrix has four possible outcomes:

Interest Group Politics. *Concentrated benefits versus concentrated harm.* An example of this circumstance was the battle starting in 2011 between banks and retailers over whether to cap the costs of debit cards. Because there is concentration of both benefits and harm among a handful of big banks and big retailers, the chance of action depends upon whether one side can gain an edge over the other. Although these conflicts create a lot of friction among the participants, it is the other three categories of conflicts that are the foundation for our current challenges.

Client Politics. *Concentrated benefits versus widely disbursed harm.* Wilson assesses the likelihood of action to be high in this case. A motivated minority actively campaigning for a favored policy regularly prevails against a majority for whom benefits are so widely dispersed that there is little motivation for anyone to advocate for action. The direct benefits of ethanol subsidies go to a relatively small number of farmers, while the costs are disbursed across all taxpayers. These concentrated beneficiaries are motivated to push aggressively for action, and because farmers represent key swing blocks in many districts, they have greater political clout. The impact on any one taxpayer is rarely enough to motivate broad opposition until outside fiscal pressures become so great that they cannot be ignored, as is currently the case.

Entrepreneurial Politics. *Widely disbursed benefits versus concentrated harm.* Reflecting the flip side of client politics, the benefits for repealing tax credits for oil and gas exploration would be widely disbursed, while the harm would be concentrated among a few oil companies. The likelihood of action is low. This case is called entrepreneurial because it would take an entrepreneur to effect change. Even though President Obama sought to be such an entrepreneur on the oil and gas tax credit issue since 2011, no change was effected due to a dedicated effort by the affected industry, confirming the difficulty of succeeding given these conditions. Client politics and entrepreneurial politics fuel the tyranny of a motivated minority. It is more difficult to address matters in the broader public interest when motivated slivers of the electorate oppose them. Therefore, energized interest groups have powerful leverage when defending their favored line in the budget from being cut and every carve-out in the tax code from being reformed.

Our Founding Fathers, with the tyranny of George III on their minds, designed our government with checks and balances to prevent a concentration of power in a king. They were also worried about the tyranny of the majority over the minority, so they discarded the idea of forming a democracy and instead created a republic to allow room for the judgment of elected officials. Eventually, they added a Bill of Rights that further protected the minority from the majority.

In that they were inventing the modern republic at the time, I suppose our Founding Fathers must be excused from not being able to anticipate that a motivated few would be able to tyrannize the indifferent many, resulting in minorities routinely trumping the will of the majority by advancing self-serving issues that collectively result in suboptimal results for the nation, as we see with client politics and entrepreneurial conditions.

Up against motivated minorities filling a member of Congress's calendar every fifteen minutes, it is hard to keep the disinterested majority at the top of one's mind.

Majoritarian Politics. *Widely distributed benefits versus widely distributed harm.* An example of this circumstance is health care or Social Security reform. Nearly everyone benefits somewhat. Nearly everyone is harmed somewhat. With so many people impacted, it is highly unlikely that action will result. The difficulty of achieving action in these conditions has contributed to the deficit and debt conditions America faces today.

The Wilson-Lowi framework gives a window into the extraordinary challenges before Congress today. In the past difficult-to-win battles with motivated minorities or majoritarian political issues could be sidestepped. Today deficit conditions and immigration policies are ratcheting up the pressure for Congress to face these very challenging issues head on.

Solution: The only solution is for leaders to level with their constituents on the need to face tough choices and to be more adept at reaching a negotiated consensus on solutions that involve truly shared sacrifices.

Actions Required

With Congress facing many hurdles to action, it is essential that robust efforts be undertaken to lower these hurdles and raise the abilities of elected officials to persuade. There are at least five actions required.

1. Advocate Balanced Redistricting

The time to start forming a robust coalition for balanced redistricting in your state in 2020 is now. It will take years to educate, strategize, and build support.

2. Reform Campaign Finance Reform

Empower candidates to ensure the most logical place for money to flow is where it will be used most responsibly and with the most accountability.

3. Bias for Action

While it may require getting elected officials to take a longer view and learn to focus on leaving a legacy of results rather than winning political contests, it is essential for them to adopt a bias for action. Too often, like in the old Tareyton cigarette advertisement, they would "rather fight than switch." Instead, they need to heed the advice of Theodore Roosevelt: "In any moment of decision the best thing you can do is the right thing, the next best thing is the wrong thing, and the worst thing you can do is nothing." It is essential to keep a focus on the need to get sixty votes in the U.S. Senate to overcome the threat of a filibuster.

While Tea Party–inspired conservatives came to office with a well-refined economic and political philosophy, they initially lacked a real philosophy of governing. "Just say no" has not engendered many good results. The maturation of leaders swept into Congress by this wave represents a necessary and positive result. The efforts by Senator Marco Rubio (R-Fla.) to drive action on immigration in the Senate was an example that this process is well under way, although he has since changed direction.

4. Don't Blame Politics, Excel at It

Too many political leaders were schooled in policy but not politics. They study how to invent perfect solutions but don't study how to come to the middle and get their hands dirty by negotiating a mutually agreeable path among competing viewpoints on the perfect solution. When they can't get their perfect, often utopian, solution implemented, they blame it on politics. In doing so, they reveal their ignorance of politics. Competing policy solutions create gridlock—one side wants to raise taxes; the other wants to cut spending. The only solution to this conflict is to get the politics right. In this sense politics trump policy. It is critical to become skilled at gathering allies with common interests and strategically advancing legislation addressing society's most pressing challenges. This effort involves a three-step process.

Select the right terrain. Successfully advancing your own agenda or thwarting misguided action begins with the vital task of strategically defining the optimal terrain upon which to engage: the question to be asked and the arena in which to ask it.

Hollywood's failed efforts to advance online piracy bills displayed the primacy of defining the question and working within the optimal arena. Traditional media players such as Comcast, News Corp, Time Warner, and Viacom sought to preserve the incentives for creativity provided by copyright protection. The legislation they supported wanted to prevent U.S. companies from placing advertisements or linking to pirating firms based outside the United States. They sought to make the question "Should U.S. companies assist foreign companies in stealing U.S. property?" and the arena to be the U.S. Congress. They lost to new electronic media outlets such as Facebook and Google that changed the question to "Do you want the federal government to blackout your Internet access?" and the arena to be that of public opinion among Internet users. Facebook and Google successfully marshaled public opinion, and the bill died before ever receiving a vote. New media redefined the question and arena. Old media lost.

Build a winning coalition. Once you have selected the right terrain, it is essential to understand that your goal must be to build a winning coalition that can appeal to a broad enough cross-section of society or political actors to prevail. This means that those who are least like you are your most valuable partners. Cookies and milk are quite different from one another, but they certainly go well together. The same is true for coalition partners. In partnering with twenty different Democrats to lead legislative initiatives during my time in Congress, I took the view that we may disagree on ninety-nine out of a hundred issues, but that shouldn't prevent us from working together on the issue upon which we agree.

Make the case. Two common mistakes encountered in making a case for action is to talk about too many messages and not talk about the right messages often enough. The U.S. oil and gas business did an excellent job of making the case when combating efforts to reduce tax incentives for exploration. When the industry CEOs were called before a congressional committee, they all stuck to the same message: incentives drove investment and innovation that sparked a natural gas production revival, which led to high-paying American jobs, cleaner sources of fuel, and greater energy independence.[5] The industry leaders understood that they needed to play an inside game (directly to elected representatives) and an outside game (to the voters), and their message was inescapable in Washington, D.C. The sector's various players echoed these refrains in billboards in Washington airports, subway stations, subway interiors, bus stops, and bus exteriors. They understood that when you are sick of repeating a message, it is just beginning to break through the clutter.[6] That sort of discipline is essential for members of Congress in today's highly contentious environment if they wish to prevail in the legislature.

5. Learn to See 360° and Speak 360°

Good politicians accentuate differences to win political campaigns. Better politicians build coalitions to move beyond agitation to action. The best politicians unify a fragmented society to pursue a common purpose. In order to be the best politician, you need to learn to See 360° and Speak 360°.

A method I use in my class is to use the example of the century-long conflict between the economic policies promulgated by John Maynard Keynes and those advocated by Friedrich von Hayek and Milton Friedman. We similarly review the competing views of foreign policy advanced by Theodore Roosevelt and Woodrow Wilson.

This approach helps students to widen their perspective and begin to See 360°.

I then have the students review speeches by national leaders to identify where they are channeling Hayek, Keynes, Roosevelt, and Wilson. They soon discover that in many cases leaders speak in the vernacular of the philosophy they adhere to but also appeal to what they perceive as the legitimate motivations of the opposing viewpoint.

While President Obama clearly embraces a Keynesian worldview, he will often give a nod to Hayek, acknowledging in his 2009 inaugural address: "Nor is the question before us whether the market is a force for good or ill. Its power to generate wealth and expand freedom is unmatched."

In a similar manner, though more an advocate of Hayek than Keynes, President George W. Bush went out of his way in his 2005 inaugural address to acknowledge those Keynesian programs he supports, saying: "In America's ideal of freedom, citizens find the dignity and security of economic independence, instead of laboring on the edge of subsistence. This is the broader definition of liberty that motivated the Homestead Act, the Social Security Act and the G.I. Bill of Rights."

You may not believe that President Bush or Obama was the best politician, but both of them did win two national elections, an extremely difficult feat. Political leaders must learn to See 360° and Speak 360° if they are to be as politically skilled as either of these presidents.

Yet presidents do not consistently appeal to all sides in all speeches. To emphasize how important it is to do so, I have my classes review four speeches: President John F. Kennedy's inaugural address, President Obama's acceptance of the Nobel Peace Prize, and the second inaugural addresses of Presidents Bush and Obama. Students find both Kennedy and Obama in Stockholm robustly appealing to both sides. In contrast, both second inaugural addresses are lopsided.

While both of the first two speeches will go down in history as being effective in their aim because everyone in the audience was made to feel as if the president addressed them directly, both second inaugurals will likely be viewed as sharpening the divide within America, as opposed to unifying a fragmented nation to pursue common interests. Political leaders must become far more skilled at appealing to all segments of society when they address our shared needs. Win-win is the only sustainable path to address the challenges we all face.

If we wish to move assertively to get past the endless standoffs we now witness in order to address our most pressing challenges, we need to actively pursue all five of these actions.

A Crisis in Democracy

The crisis in democracy is perhaps most evident from the vantage point of Asia, where the Chinese government represents a rising power and has a governing philosophy that is almost opposite that of the United States.

In 1990 the Pudong region of Shanghai boasted little more than huge piles of soybeans. Then the Chinese government decided that it wanted to make a new Manhattan there and did so in less than a decade. Sitting at a rooftop restaurant on the bund beholding the metropolis that had so quickly sprouted across the river, a U.S. investment banker said to me, "This could never have happened in a democracy like America or India."

The differences between authoritarian action and democratic gridlock are being noticed. In 2011 democracy advocates in Hong Kong resigned their posts and ran for reelection in a special election to allow the people of this formerly British, now Chinese, city to demonstrate their preference for democracy. The candidates hedged their bets up front and announced that if 25 percent of the people turned out to vote for them, it would be a reaffirmation of the populace's preference for democracy over authoritarian direction from Beijing. Despite that low bar, they nevertheless failed when only 15 percent of the people of Hong Kong turned out for their side. Pro-democracy officials later said that the result was a blow to their organization.[7]

Former Chinese premier Deng Xiaoping famously justified China's embrace of capitalism by saying: "I don't care if it's a white cat or a black cat. It's a good cat so long as it catches mice." Many in Hong Kong looked around and saw that the Beijing model of authoritarian government and capitalism were catching a lot of mice: incomes were rising, their homes were increasing in value, and the trains were running on time. They contrasted this situation with a steady stream of headlines from America of bitter partisan gridlock preventing action on widely recognized challenges and observed the Indian government's inability to reach consensus on desperately needed infrastructure investments. The residents made their preference known by staying away from the polls.

Is the lesson that we should all be more authoritarian like China? Absolutely not! China's rapid development only comes at the cost of suppressing many citizens' voices, choices, and interests. While state-controlled capitalism may appear successful in the short term as property rights are trampled in order to move forward, it inevitably leads to inefficient corruption, gross inequalities, and suppressed innovation. These challenges are increasingly becoming evident in China and may eventually sow the seeds for greater agitation for more representative government.

Even though I am confident the weaknesses of single-party authoritarianism will soon become more evident, both Indians and Americans need to realize that the real competition in government is not the other party—it is the gridlock that prevents us from tackling the issues that can lead to prosperity and peace. It is therefore incumbent on all citizens of democracy, and especially their elected officials, to embrace the needed changes outlined here and amp up their persuasion skills to find solutions to our most pressing problems and make democracy work.

NOTES

1. Nate Silver, "As Swing Districts Dwindle, Can a House Divided Stand?" *Five Thirty Eight* blog, *New York Times,* December 27, 2012, http://fivethirtyeight.blogs .nytimes.com/2012/12/27/as-swing-districts-dwindle-can-a-divided-house-stand/ (accessed on September 19, 2013).

2. Norman Dicks, "What's the Matter with Congress?" (from panel discussion, 2013 John Breaux Symposium, George Washington University, Washington, D.C., May 15, 2013).

3. Nate Garvis, with Gene Rebeck, *Naked Civics* (Plymouth, Minn.: Naked Civics, 2012).

4. David Baron, *Business and Its Environment,* 6th ed. (Upper Saddle River, N.J.: Prentice Hall College Division, 2010).

5. Richard Simon, "Oil Executives Defend Profits, Tax Cuts at Senate Hearing," *Los Angeles Times,* May 12, 2011, http://articles.latimes.com/2011/may/12/news/la-pn-oil -executives-tax-hearing-20110513 (accessed on September 19, 2013).

6. Mark Kennedy, "Social Media Provides a Megaphone for Organizations Intent on Shaping the Corporate Environment," *Emerald Strategy and Leadership* 41, no. 5 (November 2013): 39–47.

7. Joyce Woo, "Pro-Beijing Parties Sweep Hong Kong District Polls," AFP, *WebCite,* November 7, 2011, webcitation.org/63hIGlC7B (accessed on September 19, 2013).

Voices of Former Members of Congress

Former Representative Norman Dicks (D-Wash.): In the House of Representatives if you're in the minority, you recognize that the other side has the responsibility every day to put 218 votes up on the board. What I tried to do when we were in the minority after the 2010 election—I became ranking Democrat on the House Appropriations Committee—and the previous chairman and the previous ranking member had a dreadful relationship. I walked into Representative Hal Rogers's office [the ranking Republican on the committee, from Kentucky], and I said, "We cannot have this same kind of a problem, and here is what I think we should do."

Hal Rogers was completely in sync with me. As Trent Lott said, "We have got to reestablish regular order on the Appropriations Committee," and in our first year we went and took the previous year's appropriations bill, which was a continuing resolution. We probably were on the floor six or seven days—with an open rule, with over a thousand amendments—and we passed the thing.

In 2012 we passed six bills, took it from subcommittee, full committee on the House floor. We also had open rules, and we tried to establish something so that we could pass these bills and send them to the other body. Well, we sent them to the other body, and the other body didn't take up one appropriation bill, except for the continuing resolution.

I went around to every Democrat and said, "Listen, we have an interest in open rules and having a chance to offer an amendment, and so I don't want to hear anybody saying we shouldn't be cooperating with Rogers," and nobody did.

But the bottom line is there is a way to do this if you can get both sides. And it makes it much more difficult if you do all this hard work, get all this stuff done in the House of Representatives, and then see it go to the Senate and die.

Every single Democratic House member who gets elected to the Senate, I go up to them, and I tell them one thing, "You've got to change the rules in the Senate." And I say this as a former Senate staffer to Senator Warren Magnuson [D-Wash.]. I was there for eight years, from '68 to '76, the most productive time in recent history in the United States Congress. We had sixty-seven Democratic senators. No one ever thought there would be a Republican Senate. The House was overwhelmingly Democrat, and Richard Nixon was president. We passed the Clean Air Act, the Clean Water Act, the National Environmental Policy Act, created the Environmental Protection Agency. It was one of the most productive times.

Why? Because when people got here, the elections were over, and they said, "Let's work together." Every bill had a Democratic sponsor and a Republican sponsor. Every bill was basically worked out to be bipartisan, and we passed legislation. It was an amazing time.

What I see now is this bitter, hyper-partisanship that has crept into our politics. The book by Thomas Mann and Norm Ornstein, of the Brookings Institute and the American Enterprise Institute, says it perfectly: "This acrimony and hyper-partisanship have seeped into every part of the political process. Congress is deadlocked, and its approval ratings are at record lows. America's two main political parties have given up their tradition of compromise, endangering our very system of constitutional democracy. And one of these parties"—and this doesn't refer to anybody at this table because all were great leaders—"has taken on the role of insurgent outlier. The Republicans have become ideologically extreme, scornful of compromise, and ardently opposed to the established social and economic policy regime."[1]

Former Senator John Breaux (D-La.): I tried to do it when I was in the Senate, and that is the consideration of the date of our federal national elections on Tuesday.

In Louisiana all of our elections, except the presidential, are on Saturdays, so that people—many are off on Saturdays. There's nothing magical about Tuesday. It's not in the Constitution. It was simply an act of Congress that decided that we were going to have elections on Tuesday, and if you look at the history as to why the concept, it was: "Look, everybody used to go to the courthouse on Mondays to transact business. They used to go in covered wagons, so let's just have them stay over an extra day and vote on Tuesdays." So, we have Tuesday elections in almost all of the states, except my state of Louisiana.

I made the pitch to the Senate Rules Committee about moving forward with an amendment to have Congress, once again, say that elections for federal officeholders shall be on Saturdays.

I'll never forget Senator Frank Lautenberg [D-N.J.], bless him, just came unglued because Saturday being a Jewish holiday, he thought that was a terrible thing and was very strongly opposed to it. It never went anywhere, but I always thought if you're a working person who has to be at work at seven and don't get off until five, and you want to go home and rest and have dinner and have a beer, you're not going to go wait in a long line after late hours, after you had a hard day working, to sit and wait to vote.

NOTE

1. Thomas E. Mann and Norman J. Ornstein, *It's Even Worse than It Looks: How the American Constitutional System Collided with the New Politics of Extremism* (New York: Basic Books, 2012).

Contributors

Ross K. Baker is Professor of Political Science at Rutgers University. He was a Research Associate at the Brookings Institution before coming to Rutgers in 1968 and served as Chairman of the department and Graduate Director. He is the author of several books, including *Friend and Foe in the U.S. Senate; House and Senate; The New Fat Cats: Members of Congress as Political Benefactors;* and *Strangers on a Hill: Congress and the Courts.* Baker also serves on the Board of Contributors of *USA Today.* He has served on the staffs of U.S. senators Birch Bayh, Frank Church, Chuck Hagel, Patrick J. Leahy, and Walter F. Mondale and as a consultant to the Democratic Caucus of the U.S. House of Representatives. In 1992 he was a Fulbright Fellow at the Swedish Institute of International Affairs in Stockholm. Baker was Scholar-in-Residence in the Office of the Majority Leader of the United States Senate in 2008 and 2012, under Senator Harry Reid.

Mickey Edwards is Vice President of the Aspen Institute and serves as Director of the Aspen Institute's Rodel Fellowships in Public Leadership. Edwards was a Republican member of Congress from Oklahoma from 1977 to 1992. He served in the House Republican Leadership and on the Appropriations and Budget committees. After leaving Congress, he taught for eleven years at Harvard University's John F. Kennedy School of Government, where he was the John Quincy Adams Lecturer in Legislative Practice, and for five years as a lecturer at Princeton's Woodrow Wilson School of Public and International Affairs. He cochaired Citizens for Independent Courts, a task force dedicated to preserving judicial independence, and cochaired a task force on the constitutional amendment process. Edwards is the author or coauthor of four books, including, most recently, *The Parties versus the People: How to Turn Republicans and Democrats into Americans.*

Brian L. Fife is the Director of Graduate Studies as well as Professor of Public Policy in the College of Education and Public Policy at Indiana University–Purdue University Fort Wayne. His published works include *Desegregation in American Schools: Comparative Intervention Strategies; Higher Education in Transition: The Challenges of the New Millennium; Political Culture and Voting Systems in the United States: An Examination of the 2000 Presidential Election; Reforming the Electoral Process in America: Toward More Democracy in the 21st Century; School Desegregation in the Twenty-First Century: The Focus Must Change;* and most recently, *Old School Still Matters: Lessons from History to Reform Public Education in America.* His background is in political science, and his primary research interests include U.S. elections and the U.S. public education system.

Susan Herbst is the President of the University of Connecticut. Prior to her appointment as the university's fifteenth president, Herbst served as Executive Vice Chancellor and Chief Academic Officer of the University System of Georgia. Before arriving in Georgia, Herbst was Provost and Executive Vice President at the University at Albany–SUNY and also served as officer in charge of the university from 2006 to 2007. She previously served as the Dean of the College of Liberal Arts at Temple University. Herbst spent fourteen years at Northwestern University, joining the faculty in 1989 and serving in a variety of positions, including Professor of Political Science and Chair of the department. Herbst is a scholar of public opinion, media, and American politics and is the author of four books, most recently *Rude Democracy: Civility and Incivility in American Politics.*

Mark Kennedy is Professor of Political Management and Director of the Graduate School of Political Management at George Washington University. He has taught at leading universities on four continents. From 2001 to 2007 Kennedy represented Minnesota as a Republican member of the U.S. Congress, where he gained a reputation for bipartisanship. He cofounded the Economic Club of Minnesota, a platform for nonpartisan cooperation among elected officials and business leaders, and served as a presidentially appointed trade advisor under both presidents George W. Bush and Barack Obama. In business Kennedy was Senior Vice President and Treasurer of Macy's, served as the Global Retail Business Development Lead for Accenture, and formed Chartwell Strategic Advisors LLC.

Frances E. Lee is Professor of Government and Politics at the University of Maryland, where she has been a member of the faculty since 2004. She is the author of *Beyond Ideology: Politics, Principles, and Partisanship in the U.S. Senate,* which received the Richard F. Fenno Jr. Prize for the best book on legislative politics and the D. B. Hardeman Prize for the best book on Congress. She coauthored *Sizing Up the Senate: The Unequal Consequences of Equal Representation,* which also received the D. B. Hardeman Prize. She coauthors a comprehensive textbook on the U.S. Congress, *Congress and Its Members,* which is regularly updated to reflect changes in the House and Senate. Her articles have appeared in *American Journal of Political Science, American Political Science Review, Journal of Politics,* and *Legislative Studies Quarterly,* among others. She was a Research Fellow at the Brookings Institution from 1997 to 1998 and an APSA Congressional Fellow from 2002 to 2003. From 1998 to 2003 she taught in the Department of Political Science at Case Western Reserve University.

Robert Mann holds the Manship Chair in Journalism at the Manship School of Mass Communication at Louisiana State University in

Baton Rouge. He served as press secretary to U.S. senators Russell Long and John Breaux, both Democrats from Louisiana. He is the author of critically acclaimed political histories of the U.S. civil rights movement, the Vietnam War, and American wartime dissent. His most recent book, *Daisy Petals and Mushroom Clouds: LBJ, Barry Goldwater, and the Ad That Changed American Politics,* was named by the *Washington Post* as one of the best political books of 2011. He is also a political columnist for the *New Orleans Times-Picayune.*